Mosaics: Hobby and Art

MOSAICS:

Hobby and Art

EDWIN A. HENDRICKSON

HILL AND WANG · NEW YORK

TO MY MOTHER AND FATHER

Preface

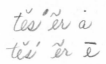

From the very beginnings of what archeologists term "civilization," when man began to specialize and build, his desire to create and achieve aesthetically almost always included the medium of mosaics.

In the valleys of the Tigris and Euphrates rivers in Asia Minor the ruins of the ancient lost civilizations of the Sumerians and Chaldaeans reveal lovely mosaics both in architectural use and in furniture and jewelry. These ancient civilizations and their art including mosaics are dated at about 3600 B.C.

The early fragments were usually made of precious and colorful stones placed in random patterns into wood, bone, and ivory. From this there developed the use of the stones in close placement to each other to form designs and actual pictures and designs. When the base material to hold the "stones" became part of the structure, mosaics as we know them today came into being.

As new civilizations emerged new developments in the use of the "stones" came into being. The Egyptians and Greeks, followed by the Romans, perfected techniques and uses of art forms. To achieve greater vibrancy and subtlety in color range, the pieces, or tesserae, were manufactured from glass and ceramics, rather than using just natural materials such as pieces of marble and stones.

The Greeks made innovations in the art forms of mosaic by breaking away from the prevalent use of the geometric forms. They began making mosaics of pastoral scenes on walls and floors; the colors were generally black, white, natural stone, and pastel shades.

Use of texture in laying the mosaics to achieve shadow and light and dimensional forms was developed to a high degree by Roman artists. Brightly colored glass, known today as Byzantine and Italian glass tesserae, was used in great abundance for murals, walls, and floors in public buildings.

The influence of Christianity and the church in Italy initiated the use of mosaics in church interiors. Figures in brilliant colors, laid in solid gold backgrounds, were used extensively. The mosaic artists mastered their craft so well during this period that from a distance many mosaics seem like painted murals. The trend in mosaics was toward greater realism and away from geometrical designs, texture, and the natural quality of the "stones." The beauty of the stone and the integrity of the material itself in some ways became lost. Mosaics became like mural paintings, and stones were used like bits of paint.

By the sixteenth century the magnificent murals by Italian artists had reduced the interest in mosaics to formal classic forms in the great cathedrals. When almost photographic realism was accomplished by

vii

artists, their interest in the medium died. Craftsmen rather than artists kept the ancient art in existence, but they did little in the way of artistic innovations.

While painting and murals were going through various artistic revolutions, such as impressionism, abstract, and nonobjective periods, mosaics remained almost untouched as an artistic medium.

In the last few years new interest in mosaics has developed and new forms in mosaics are being used by contemporary art masters. Already some fine artistic mosaics are beginning to appear in the United States. Exciting and beautiful mosaics can be seen on some public buildings in Mexico—the most notable example is the breath-taking Aztec-like mosaic on the University of Mexico Library in Mexico City.

Mosaics as a hobby is very recent. In the older civilizations in Europe and Asia, mosaic work and art was done by artisans and guild-craft unions. The tricks of the trade, the methods, equipment, and materials were passed down from generation to generation, from father to son, or from artisan to his apprentice. Likewise, mosaics in America were first done by European craftsmen, and often their methods, equipment, and sources of supply were closely guarded trade secrets.

During the 1930's some American artists began using mosaics as an art form, principally under the WPA Art Projects. For the most part, these artists continued to use the methods of the Italians, which is much too laborious for most amateurs. It was not until after World War II, when American tourists returned from vacations in Italy, where they had seen the beauty of the Venetian, the Roman, and other mosaics in the cathedrals, that a strong interest was born. Questions arose as to how to make mosaics, what materials to use, and where to obtain supplies.

Mosaic for hobby use was not considered by the individual American craftsmen developing techniques for making mosaics. The new methods were being developed for the manufacture of finished furniture and murals which could be marketed in furniture and decorator showrooms. The price of these lovely and practical mosaics naturally was exorbitant.

Mr. Hans Scharff, of the Scharff Trading Company, was one of the first to develop methods for making mosaic furniture in this country. Mr. John Stewart, of Stewart Studio, Mr. Nicholas Argiro, of Mosaic Arts, and others developed methods of their own, but again the hobby possibilities were not considered. Contrariwise, to a considerable degree these artists guarded their particular methods as carefully as manufacturers protect their patents.

The author and Miss Laura Beaujon of Mosaic Crafts began developing methods, testing the strength of materials, and how to use mosaics artistically in furniture, in 1954. Some of the techniques developed were simple and structurally sound, if used with the proper materials and equipment. There was an immediate strong interest from people acquainted with the experiments. The author and Miss Beaujon decided to make up detailed instructions and several very simple mosaic kits and introduce them in their store. Interest materialized immediately, and other hobby stores began to carry mosaic supplies. Now anyone can make beautiful and useful mosaics.

Another most fascinating American innovation is *Mosaialight,* which was discovered during the early experiments by the author, with Miss Laura Beaujon and Mr. Hjalmer H. Boyesen. While experimenting with various backings and colors of the Italian glass tesserae, it was noticed that the tesserae were somewhat translucent. This translucent quality, when combined with proper back lighting and proper mounting, gives forth a beautiful glow, more subtle and delicate than stained glass.

The problems of making *Mosaialight* practical were eventually overcome through long research into backings, adhesives, and cements. Ordinary backings and adhesives, because of their inherent qualities in regard to strength and temperature, were found to be inadequate. The coefficients of expansion between different materials, such as the Italian glass tesserae, an inert material, and its backing which, when heated, expands, posed special problems.

Research-tested methods and materials were eventually developed for *Mosaialight* (patent pending). Permission for its use, and instructions, can be obtained by writing to the author in care of the publisher.

In this book we introduce practical methods of constructing mosaics, uses of materials, qualities of materials, artistic techniques, and other information that is important to the mastery of mosaics as a hobby and art.

Acknowledgments

The author is especially indebted to the following two consulting artists:

John Kidder

Carmine D'Avino

Their advice, assistance, and actual finished mosaics were invaluable in the preparation of this book.

The author is also indebted to the following artists for their advice, cooperation, and actual mosaic work reproduced in this book: James Dorris, Clements Gregory, Jack Gregory, Donald Schenker, Alice Olson, Larry Argiro, Jon Suzuki, Kenneth Weiss, Hans Scharff, Valerie Clairbout, David Holloman, Samuel Kaner, Hjalmer H. Boyeson, George Morrison, and Dolores Onarato.

A considerable amount of time and preparation was necessary for the layout and completion of the projects. For this, sincere appreciation is expressed to the following: Laura Beaujon, Harold Merriam, Tetsuya Kochi, Richard Swift, Vivian Newberg, Lois MacGregor, Rhoda Large, Alida Berling, Marc Vincent, and Barbara Chapin.

The photographic work was possible through the assistance and cooperation of Albert Schaler, Laura Beaujon, Melvin Mills, Lennie Lencina, the Lawrence Studio, Dennis Purse, and Larry Argiro of State Teachers College, New Paltz, N. Y.

The author is indebted to specialists in several fields for their technical advice: Louis Goldey on Italian tesserae; George Asch on bases and Italian tesserae; Asa Clark on bases and carpentry; Boyan Alesh on wrought iron and brass; Hans Scharff and Mrs. Lucy Steele on the background of American techniques and methods of setting tesserae; and Ralph Treves for editorial advice. The author is also grateful to Myrtle Powell for her assistance in putting all the material together.

E.A.H.

April, 1957

Contents

page

Preface   vii

PART 1: PROJECTS

Project 1 Trivet   3
   2 Stacking Table   5
   3 Mosaic-edged Shelves   8
   4 Hot Plate or Paperweight   10
   5 Cylindrical Lamp Base   12
   6 Brass Tray or Wall Hanging   14
   7 End Table   17
   8 Round Sunburst Coffee Table   20
   9 Book Ends   27
   10 Oval Sunburst Coffee Table   31
   11 Ash Tray or Wall Hanging   37
   12 Ceramic Swimming Pool Table   40

PART 2: MATERIALS AND METHODS

Chapter 1 Kinds of Tesserae   45
   2 Cutting and Shapping Tesserae   53
   3 Backings, Edgings, and Hardware   57
   4 Adhesives   64
   5 Cements and Dyes   67
   6 Direct and Indirect Methods of Application   72
   7 How to Design a Mosaic   75
   8 Mosaic Walls and Panels   80
   9 Mosaic Floors and Walks   87

PART 3: PATTERNS

Pattern 1 Abstract Girl   91
   2 Star and Spiral Tray   92
   3 Pomegranate Tree   93
   4 Star and Sphinx Wall Hanging   94
   5 Indian Design Coffee Table   95
   6 Sunburst Tray   96
   7 Tulip Tray   96
   8 The Man   97
   9 Prancing Horse   98
   10 Flying Bird Tray   99
   11 Mosaialight Abstract   100
   12 Nude   101
   13 Woman's Face   102

14 Fish Abstract   103
15 Free Form Logo of a "Home Show"   104
16 Abstract   105
17 The Birds   106
18 Greek Key Coffee Table   107
19 Fruit Bowl Abstract   108
20 Cat   109

Sources of Supply   111

Mosaics: Hobby and Art

PART 1:   Projects

Projects

We use certain terms in these projects which need brief definitions. Mosaic is the term given to the finished piece of work—the table top, the wall hanging, and other art objects.

Tessera, a single piece, and tesserae, more than one piece, are used to define the small pieces of hard material used in laying a mosaic surface. We make a further distinction by giving the specific name for the tesserae, for example: Italian glass tesserae, Italian ceramic tesserae, marble tesserae, Japanese porcelain tesserae.

We have noted in the projects whether they utilize the direct method of application or the indirect method of application. These methods are fully discussed in a later section; in the projects we give step-by-step instructions necessary to the making of the object.

In the chapters following the projects we fully describe the materials, equipment, and methods for doing mosaic work—helpful to those who wish to design their own mosaics or to work from the patterns included.

Hot Plate or Trivet

This simple project, using the direct method of application, will make a beautiful and useful hot plate. It may also be used as a paperweight, coaster, or decoration.

Equipment and Supplies

1. One wrought-iron angle iron frame 4½″ square, lacquered black, or 4 pieces of angle-shaped wood picture molding mitered at the ends.
2. One square of ⅛″ thick masonite or pressed board, cut to fit the frame.
3. Two-ounce tube of mosaic adhesive.
4. Twelve white and 13 black Italian glass tesserae.
5. One-half pound of mosaic cement, ceramic grout, or a mixture of Portland cement (1 part cement to 2 to 3 parts fine white sand).
6. Silicone polish.
7. Four strips of sheet cork.
8. Masking tape 1″ wide.
9. Cloth pad and copper scouring pad.
10. Mixing bowl.
11. Sponge or cloth.

Instructions

1. If using the picture molding, glue the pieces together with Elmer's Glue or some other carpenter's adhesive.
2. Put a ribbon of mosaic adhesive around inside bottom of the frame. Place masonite square into the frame, smooth side up. Put masking tape around edges of the frame to protect from cement stains.

3. Soak tesserae loose from the paper backing. Soak in warm water to remove any foreign matter. Wipe dry.
4. Squeeze a ribbon of mosaic adhesive onto the masonite along left edge, working

down from top left corner. Place a black tessera, ridged side down, into the adhesive at upper left corner. Next to it, along the left edge, place a white tessera—then black, white, and black. The smooth side of Italian tesserae is always the top, and the beveled ridged side is always the under side.

5. Space the tesserae in the first row by moving gently with forefinger or a toothpick.

6. Squeeze a ribbon of the adhesive into the next row. Place tesserae, starting with a white one at the top. Space, as in step 5. Repeat process until all 25 tesserae are glued into place.

7. Wait 8 to 20 hours (often depends upon the weather) until the adhesive is dry and firmly holding the tesserae. Test by trying to move the tesserae with your finger.

8. When adhesive is dry, prepare cement. Put it in a mixing bowl. Add water, pouring

it down side of the bowl a little at a time while stirring slowly with a spoon or with your hand. Mix until cement is smooth and the consistency of very heavy pancake batter. With your hand rub the cement over the mosaic, working it into the spaces between the tesserae. Clean the cement off the surface of the tesserae with a dry cloth, being careful not to scoop out any from between them. Let dry 45 to 90 minutes.

9. With a sponge or cloth clean the trivet top and edges. If necessary, scrub top with copper scouring pad or scrape any excess cement from the top of the mosaic with a penknife.

10. To waterproof the cement between the tesserae, rub mosaic with silicone marble polish.

11. Glue the four thin strips of sheet cork to the bottom of the trivet, or at the four corners.

Stacking Table

This simple project, using the indirect method of application, makes a useful strong and attractive wrought-iron table 12″ square and 16″ high. Made of Asian porcelain tesserae, it may be used in or outdoors.

Equipment and Supplies

1. One wrought-iron angle frame, lacquered black, 12¾″ square with 16″ wrought-iron legs welded to each corner. The frame's 12¾″ outside measurement allows 12″ on the inside for the tesserae.
2. One square of ⅛″ thick masonite or pressed board, cut to fit exactly inside the frame—usually 12¼″ square.
3. Tube of mosaic adhesive or a can of ceramic adhesive.
4. Three fourths to one pound of mosaic cement, Miracle tile grout, or a mixture of Portland cement (1 part cement to 2 to 3 parts fine white sand).
5. One square foot of Asian porcelain tesserae, pasted face down on paper.
6. Four plastic feet to slip onto the ends of the wrought-iron legs.
7. Mixing bowl.
8. Masking tape 1″ wide.
9. Sponge or cloth.
10. Shellac and brush.
11. Silicone polish.

Instructions

1. Spread newspapers on floor beneath table frame.
2. Shellac masonite square on both sides.
3. Put a ribbon of the adhesive around the inside top of the frame. Place masonite into the frame, rough side up. Make certain it comes into contact with the adhesive on all sides.
4. Place masking tape around outside

5

top edge of the frame to protect the paint while working.

5. When the adhesive is holding the masonite firmly (½ to 3 hours), wet the rough side of masonite with a sponge.

6. Check sheet of tesserae to see that all pieces are attached to the paper and are face down. If any have become loose, glue them back in place with Duco cement or a water solvent flour paste. With paper side down, bottom side of tesserae up, wet tesserae with a sponge. Do this until they are dampened thoroughly.

7. Place masking tape around underside edges of frame to avoid cement leakage.

8. Put cement in a bowl. Add water, pouring it down side of bowl a little at a time while stirring slowly with a spoon or with your hand. Mix until cement is smooth and is the consistency of very heavy pancake batter.

9. Pour three fourths of the cement evenly over the entire surface of the masonite.

10. Redampen bottom side of the tesserae. Place the entire sheet, paper side up, bottom side of tesserae down, into the wet cement. Push the paper and tesserae around until the paper is evenly spaced within the frame. Push down firmly with your hand until the paper surface is level with table top edge. Starting in the center, with the flat of your hand rub out to the edges of the paper sheet, squeezing any excess cement out over the edges. Continue until the top is perfectly level.

11. Let the cement set for a few minutes. With a wet cloth or sponge thoroughly dampen paper holding the tesserae together. Let paper soak for a few minutes. Holding one edge of the paper between thumb and forefinger, pull up the paper, removing in one piece, if possible, or in long strips. If paper continues to adhere to the tesserae, sponge it again, but do not dilute cement with too much water, as this may weaken the consistency of the cement. If individual pieces pull up with the paper, push down into place in the cement after you have removed the paper.

12. Straighten any pieces that are out of line. Equalize surface around any that are pushed down too far by gently rubbing hand over area around tesserae. If this does not level surface, pry up piece, place a bit more cement into area, and replace. Fill in any areas between tesserae with more cement, redampening it if necessary, until cracks between are filled level with tesserae.

13. Place a matting of dampened newspaper over the entire top and let cement dry gradually, usually 8 to 10 hours. The matting prevents cement from drying too quickly and becoming powdery.

14. When cement is dry, wipe off the chalky film surface with damp cloth or sponge. If cement spots remain on tesserae, dampen surface thoroughly and rub with fine steel wool. Clean off, and wipe dry. Waterproof cement between tesserae with silicone polish.

15. Remove masking tape from the frame. Clean off any adhesive or foreign matter with lighter fluid.

16. To place plastic feet onto table legs, drop a bit of glue into the right angle slots of feet, then slide onto ends of legs.

Mosaic-edged Shelves

Italian glass tesserae edging gives a finished and unusual appearance to ordinary shelves, and provides a touch of color that can be pleasing. Made by the direct method.

Equipment and Supplies

1. Three pieces of ¾″ thick exterior grade plywood, 36″x12″.
2. Six metal wall brackets 9″ to 10″ in length.
3. Twelve ¾″ round head steel screws, and 12 cement nails or long screws for attaching shelf brackets to wall.
4. Italian glass tesserae, ¾″ square: 230 pieces in any color or color combination desired.
5. Mosaic cutter.
6. Two-ounce tube of mosaic adhesive.
7. One pound of mosaic cement.
8. Shellac and brush.
9. Masking tape 1″ wide.
10. Mixing bowl.
11. Sponge or cloth.

Instructions

1. If you wish to do the shelves in a pattern of full and some half mosaics, to break the symmetry of the ¾″ size, cut the desired number of mosaics in half with a mosaic cutter. Place the cutter edge in from the edge of the tessera about ⅛″ and give a sharp snip.
2. Place the three pieces of plywood on a working surface, with newspaper underneath. Shellac edges and tops of shelves. Let dry thoroughly.
3. Place ribbon of adhesive on front and side edges of shelves. Let dry for several minutes. Put on another ribbon of adhesive, so that it is fairly thick. In several minutes the adhesive should be slightly tacky. Following your color and design pattern, place

8

tesserae onto the adhesive, beveled side down, around entire front and side shelf edge. Repeat on remaining shelves.

4. Place strip of masking tape over mosaic edge of each shelf. Let adhesive dry 30 to 48 hours; then remove masking tape.

5. Put cement in mixing bowl. Add water, pouring it down side of the bowl a little at a time, and mix in with a spoon or with your hand until it is the consistency of very heavy pancake batter. Let stand for a few minutes. With your hand rub the cement over the tesserae, working it into the spaces between them. Continue until all the spaces are filled.

6. Clean the cement off the surface of the tesserae with a dry cloth, being careful not to scoop out any from between them. Let dry 8 to 12 hours.

7. With a damp cloth or sponge, clean the tesserae until the surface is completely clean.

8. Attach brackets to bottom of shelves about 4″ in from the ends with ¾″ round head steel screws.

9. Attach shelves to wall with cement nails or long screws.

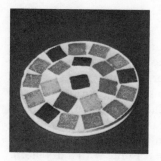

Hot Plate or Paperweight

Made from a discarded coffee-tin lid, by the direct method, this item is inexpensive. A set of these makes an attractive gift.

Equipment and Supplies

1. Lid removed from a coffee tin, 4″ in diameter and with lip ¼″ deep.
2. Paint remover or a knife.
3. Twenty-one Italian glass tesserae.
4. Two-ounce tube of mosaic adhesive.
5. One-half pound of mosaic cement, tile grout, or a mixture of Portland cement (1 part cement to 2 to 3 parts fine white sand).
6. Mixing bowl.
7. Cloth.
8. Steel or copper scouring pads.
9. Furniture wax, preferably liquid with silicone base.
10. Clear lacquer and brush.

Instructions

1. Spread newspaper to work on. Remove paint from lid with paint remover, or scrape off with a knife. Wash lid and dry.

2. Place thin ribbon of adhesive around inside of ¼″ lip. Squeeze another thin ribbon of adhesive next to first, around inside. For this project, if mosaic adhesive is not available use Elmer's Glue, Duco, or some other strong household adhesive. Lighter fluid will remove any adhesive from the hands.

3. Place a tessera bevel side down into the adhesive. Push with finger until two corners of outer edge of the tessera touch the rim. Place second tessera next to the first. Continue with the tesserae until the entire outer circle is completed. Thirteen tesserae should be sufficient.

4.   Squeeze adhesive over remaining inside lid area.

5.   Place one tessera in the exact center. Space seven tesserae around it, as shown in completed trivet.

6.   Push tesserae around gently with forefinger to arrange symmetrically. Let adhesive dry 12 hours.

7.   Put cement in bowl. Add water, pouring it down side of the bowl a little at a time, and mix with a spoon or with your hand until it is the consistency of very heavy pancake batter.

8.   Pour cement over and between tesserae. Wipe excess cement from top of mosaic with your hand or a slightly damp cloth, being careful not to scoop any from between the tesserae. Let dry 8 to 12 hours.

9.   Pour water over the top and scrub off any remaining cement, using steel or copper scouring pads if necessary. When clean, let dry.

10.   Polish mosaic with furniture wax.

11.   Lacquer the tin base and outer rim.

Cylindrical Lamp Base

The rough, uneven surface of the Byzantine tesserae used in making this project, by the direct method, reflects light and gives a brilliant touch to any setting. This decorator lamp base would cost well over $100 if purchased ready-made.

Equipment and Supplies

1. A round wooden cylinder 5¾" in diameter and 14½" high. If made from a solid block, have a hole ⅜" to ½" in diameter drilled through the center for the electrical cord.
2. A round wooden disc of walnut, mahogany or birch 6" in diameter and ½" thick, with a hole through center to match that in base.
3. A round disc of thick matted cork 5½" in diameter and 1/16" thick; also with matching hole through center.
4. Approximately five pounds of Byzantine tesserae. Plan your design, if any, and colors wanted, before purchasing.
5. Five-ounce tube of mosaic adhesive.
6. Carpenter's glue, such as Elmer's or Rivet.
7. Sandpaper.
8. Shellac and brush.
9. Linseeed oil, tung oil, or furniture wax.
10. Electrical attachments: socket, cord, and plug.

Instructions

Note: If a wooden cylinder is difficult to find, you may use a cylinder of stovepipe or heavy cardboard. However, in this case the bottom and top discs must be attached very securely, and sand or some other heavy material placed inside the cylinder to give it weight and hold the attachments in place. Otherwise, the lamp will be top-heavy.

1. Sand the edge of the 6" wooden disc until smooth.
2. Smear carpenter's glue on the top of the cylinder and the bottom of the 6" disc. Press disc down onto cylinder, matching the holes for the cord. Place weight on top of disc. Leave for 6 to 8 hours, or until glue has had time to harden.
3. Turn base upside down, smear glue on bottom of cylinder. Press cork disc onto cylinder, matching the holes for the cord. Let it dry.

4. Place lamp base upright. Shellac around cylinder from top to bottom. Let dry 20 to 30 minutes. This prevents the mosaic adhesive from soaking into the base, which would weaken its adhesive power in holding the tesserae.

5. Draw or transfer your design onto the cylinder, using a color code, if you wish, to indicate color in each area.

6. Spread out tesserae and separate by color, ready for use.

7. Place lamp base on its side. Starting at the top, spread mosaic adhesive around the base until it covers a strip 4″ from the top. Apply rather thickly. Let dry slightly, until it becomes tacky.

8. Following your design, place each peace of tesserae, uneven cut side out, into adhesive around base. Adjust pieces by pushing with forefinger, but do not leave space between; set pieces next to each other.

9. Repeat steps 7 and 8 until the cylinder is covered with the tesserae.

10. Let adhesive dry from 30 to 50 hours.

11. Check to make certain all the pieces are firmly held in place. Test by running forefinger over each of the rows of tesserae. Pry out any loose pieces, reapply adhesive, let dry until tacky, and replace tesserae.

12. Give the wooden disc on the top a beautiful finish with applications of linseed oil, tung oil, or furniture wax, repeated over several days, and again in a few weeks.

13. Pull cord down through cylinder. Make socket secure at top. Attach plug to end of cord.

Brass Tray or Wall Hanging

Using the direct method, this polished and lacquered tray of brass and Italian tesserae makes a useful tray or a colorful wall hanging.

Equipment and Supplies

1. A polished brass tray 11½" in diameter, with a hanger on the back. It should be lacquered, and it will probably have a satin finish on the back. It must have a flat center of 7½" in diameter, with a polished edge tapering upward for approximately 2¼".
2. Italian glass tesserae chips: ½ lb. white and off-white-gray; ¼ lb. black; ⅛ lb. orange; ⅛ lb. gold dust; ⅛ lb. light aqua blue.
3. Two-ounce tube of mosaic adhesive.
4. One-half pound of mosaic cement.
5. Paper shopping bag 15" to 16" long and 12" wide.
6. Masking tape 1" wide.
7. Copper scouring pads or steel wool.
8. Silicone marble polish or silicone waterproofing compound.
9. Mixing bowl and sponge.
10. Scissors.

Instructions

1. Slide brass tray into shopping bag and trace outline around the 7½" flat center. Remove tray. Draw a second circle around outside of this outline, ¼" to ½" away, to increase size of circle. Cut out around second circle.
2. Place tray in shopping bag with inside center of tray exposed through the hole. Place masking tape around inside of tray at

edge of 7½" flat center where it starts tapering upward, catching the cut edge of the
shopping bag also and pressing it down to
the tray. This protects the polished lacquered rim of the tray from the adhesive
and cement.

3.   Wipe clean the exposed flat part of
the tray.

4.   Spread the tesserae chips by color beside the shopping bag, ready
to use.

5.   Following the above picture of the completed tray, draw a rough
sketch of the fish onto the center of the brass tray with a pencil, or
scratch it in with the point of a penknife. The fish is of abstract design, so your sketch need not be accurate. Draw lines through the fish
dividing it into 5 vertical parts, and mark colors to go in them as follows: black chips in the head area, with a thin gold-dust mouth and
eye; aqua blue in the next area; then orange; then gold dust; then a
black tail, and black fins. The background area is a blending of the
white and off-white gray chips.

6.   Starting with the head area of the fish, spread a ribbon of mosaic adhesive, place the black and the gold chips face up, ridged side
down, into the adhesive. Move the pieces about until they are suitably
arranged. Put down the adhesive in the next section and arrange the
aqua blue chips; then continue with the orange, then the gold dust,
then the black in the tail area and in the fins. When the fish is filled
in and arranged in a pleasing manner, spread a ribbon of adhesive
around the fish, and fill in with the white and off-white gray chips.
Place them closely to the fish; since the adhesive dries slowly, you can
adjust the tesserae by pushing with your forefinger until they are well
placed. Then continue with the adhesive and chips until all the background area is covered. If some chips do not seem to fit as you wish
them to, pry out with a toothpick, and replace with more desirable
ones.

7.   Remove any adhesive that has oozed up or gotten on top of the
chips. If the adhesive has dried, apply a bit of lighter fluid to soften,
then peel off with a penknife or toothpick.

8.   Let adhesive dry 12 to 35 hours. Then test by running the flat of
your hand over the surface. The tesserae should not move from the
pressure of your hand.

9.   Put cement in bowl and mix gradually with water until it is the
consistency of very heavy pancake batter. Mix thoroughly. (Too much
water in the mixture weakens the cement and makes it prone to staining.)

10.   Pour one fourth to one half of the cement onto the tesserae. With
your hand or a dry cloth rub the cement over the entire surface, forcing

it into the cracks. Add more cement if necessary, and rub until all the spaces are filled. Let stand for several minutes to permit cement to settle. If surface is not smooth and even, add more cement. Let stand 5 to 10 minutes. Wipe excess cement from the surface but do not try to clean thoroughly. Wait 20 minutes to one hour, and then wipe clean with a dry cloth, leaving a very thin film of chalky cement. Let dry 4 to 8 hours.

11.   Wet surface and scrub clean with a sponge or wet cloth. If any of cement film remains, scrub with copper scouring pads or steel wool. If steel wool is used, remove all the minute steel particles, or they may rust and stain the cement. Let tray dry for several hours.

12.   Waterproof cement with a coat of liquid silicone marble polish or silicone waterproofing compound.

13.   Remove masking tape and slide tray from the shopping bag.

14.   With a dry clean cloth wipe any foreign matter from the brass edge. If any of the lacquer has chipped, touch up with clear lacquer, using a small watercolor paint brush.

End Table

Table top of Italian tesserae in a Mondrian design, using the direct method of application, and with a mahogany or walnut edge. Overall 14¼" x 24". Without legs, this makes a practical tray or wall hanging.

Equipment and Supplies

1. A piece of ¾" thick exterior grade plywood, 14"x24".
2. Two strips of mahogany or walnut edging ⅛" thick, ⅞" wide and 14¼" long.
3. Two strips of same edging 24" long.
4. Four brass, wood or wrought-iron legs, 15" to 20" high, depending upon your preference.
5. Four slant or straight flanges into which the legs are screwed.
6. Sixteen ¾" No. 7 round head steel screws.
7. Carpenter's glue.
8. Clamps.
9. Finishing nails.
10. Sandpaper.
11. Clear shellac and brush.
12. Wood finishing oils, and wax.
13. Masking tape 1" wide.
14. Five-ounce tube of mosaic adhesive.
15. Three pounds of mosaic cement or a mixture of Portland cement (1 part cement to 2 to 3 parts marble dust or fine white sand).
16. Italian glass tesserae ¾" square: 18 light blue, 30 red, 21 yellow, 45 orange, 379 white.
17. Silicone marble polish.
18. Mixing bowl, scouring pads and cloths.

Instructions

1. Place the piece of plywood on a flat working surface. Apply a strong carpenter's glue to the ends. Place the two short pieces of edging

17

into the glue, flush with bottom of plywood and approximately ¼″ higher than plywood surface. Clamp. Apply glue along sides, put longer pieces of edging into glue so they butt joint up to the end pieces. Clamp. Finishing nails may be used instead of glue to hold edging on; they should be countersunk and puttied over when finishing the edging. Let glue dry 8 to 12 hours, until edging is firmly held to the plywood. Sand the edges.

2. Cover the edging with masking tape. Apply a thin brush coat of clear shellac to both top and bottom of plywood. Let dry.

3. Lay out the tesserae by color. Follow diagram in placing tesserae. They will fill in the design as follows: upper left rectangle, 30 red; upper right rectangle, 21 yellow; lower right rectangle, 45 orange; the two squares, each 9 light blue; remaining areas, 379 white.

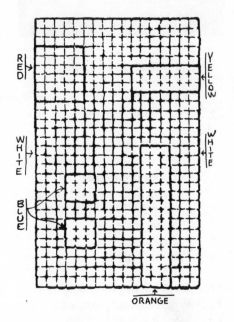

4. Squeeze a ribbon of mosaic adhesive along the left side. Working down from top left corner, place a white tessera, beveled ridged side down, into the adhesive. Repeat this down the side toward you until the white tesserae are all in place. Space them evenly with your forefinger. Squeeze a ribbon of adhesive into the next row; place white tesserae and space evenly. When you come to the color areas, place the tesserae as indicated in the design. Continue placing them, spacing satisfactorily, until the table top is filled.

5. Let the adhesive dry 20 to 40 hours. Then test by running the flat of your hand over the surface. The tesserae should not move from the pressure of your hand.

6. When adhesive is dry, prepare cement. Put approximately 2¾ lbs. into a mixing bowl. Add water, pouring it down side of bowl a little at a time while stirring slowly with a spoon or with your hand. Mix until cement is smooth and the consistency of very heavy pancake batter.

7. Pour about three fourths of the mixed cement over the mosaic. Spread cement until it covers the entire surface. With either your hand or a cloth rub the cement vigorously, working it into the cracks. Add more cement if necessary, and rub until all the spaces are filled. Let stand 3 to 5 minutes to permit cement to settle. Wipe excess cement

from surface, being careful not to scoop
cement from between the tesserae. Do not
try to clean thoroughly at this time. Let
stand 20 to 30 minutes.

8.   With a slightly damp cloth wipe surface again so that it is clean of all cement,
except for a chalky film. With the extra cement, fill in any spaces or holes between the
pieces which may have developed in the drying process. The excess cement left in your mixing bowl can be made reworkable by dampening
slightly and then kneading a lump of it in the palm of the hand. Let dry
8 to 12 hours.

9.   Sponge off the chalky film with water. If it does not come off
easily, wet surface and scrub vigorously with copper scouring pads;
scrape with a penknife if necessary. When clean, dry the surface.

10.   To waterproof the cement between the tesserae, rub with a small
amount of liquid silicone marble polish.

11.   Turn table top over and stain the bottom with a wood stain, pouring a small
amount onto the plywood and spreading it
over the entire surface with a lint-free cloth.
Let it soak into the plywood, then wipe off
any excess stain.

12.   Attach the four flanges, one in each
corner of the underside. Place straight
flanges in approximately ¾″ to 1″ from the
corners, mark through with a pencil for
screw holes. Remove flanges. With hammer
and nail, or an electric drill, make small
holes at the pencil points. Place flanges
back over holes, one flange at a time, and

attach with ¾″ round head steel screws. Start screws with a light tap
of a hammer, then screw flanges down firmly. If you are using slanted
legs, place the slant flanges in farther from the corners, so that the legs
will not protrude beyond the edges of the table. Screw legs tightly into
the flanges.

13.   Turn table right side up and peel masking tape from the edging.
Smooth the edging with fine sandpaper. Oil with linseed or tung oil.
Repeat oil application over several days, then repeat once a week for
two or three weeks, to give the table a nice finish.

14.   When the wood is well oiled, apply a coating of furniture wax
and polish.

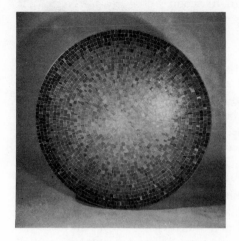

Round Sunburst Coffee Table

A brass-edged table of Pelv Italian glass tesserae applied by the indirect method, and with a smooth stainproof top impervious to damage. In a furniture showroom this table costs four times the cost of materials.

Equipment and Supplies

1. A circle of ¾" thick exterior grade plywood, 36" diameter.
2. A strip of 1/16" to 1/25" brass, 1" to 2" in width, 10' long.
3. Tin snips, file for metal, 2 metal clamps.
4. Small block of hard asbestos.
5. Brazing flux.
6. Small blow torch (Prepo brand is adequate), 6" strip or coil of silver solder.
7. Leather gloves.
8. Emery or sandpaper, steel wool.
9. Shellac, clear lacquer, and small brush.
10. Wood stain, brass polish.
11. Three brass coated 16" hollow steel legs, and plastic tips for legs.
12. Three slant flanges.
13. Twelve ¾" round head steel wood screws.
14. Masking tape 1" wide.
15. Pelv Italian glass tesserae as follows: 2¼ sq. ft. No. 188 DI, bone black; 2 sq. ft. No. 137C, very dark gray; 1¾ sq. ft. No. 124B, dark gray; 1 sq. ft. No. 122A, medium gray; ½ sq. ft. No. 120A, light gray; ¼ sq. ft. No. 119A, white.
16. One five-ounce and one two-ounce tube of glass mosaic adhesive.
17. Eight to nine pounds of mosaic cement.
18. Small amount of bone black mineral pigment.
19. Two medium-sized tubes of Duco cement.
20. Mosaic cutter.
21. A square of kraft wrapping paper 40"x40".
22. Copper scouring pads.

23.   Large mixing bowl, rolling pin, cloths.
24.   Silicone marble polish.

Instructions

1.   If possible, purchase plywood circle with brass edging already attached, or have a sheet metal worker place the brass stripping around the plywood.

2.   If you are a home carpenter, you may perform this difficult task yourself. Place the plywood circle on your workroom floor, then stretch brass around the outside until it is taut. Mark brass strip with a nail or pencil where it meets (do not allow for an overlap). The strip must make a perfect fit around the plywood circle when butted together. Remove strip from around plywood, Using a square, draw a line across brass where marked. Measure and mark off with the square another line $\frac{1}{8}''$ to $\frac{1}{4}''$ inside the first line, so the strip will be just short of making a perfect butt fit when stretched around the plywood.

3.   Cut with tin snips on the second line drawn. File cut end with a metal file so that it will make a clean butt with the other end.

4.   Place the small block of asbestos at the end corner of your workbench. With a metal clamp, fasten one end of the brass stripping, in about 2″ from the end, to the asbestos block. Clamp the other end in the same manner and so that the two ends of brass are perfectly butted together (not overlapping or one end higher than the other).

5.   Spread brazing flux over the area between the two clamps and where the two ends meet. Light the blow torch according to its instructions, and slowly adjust to a hot flame. Semidarken the room so you can more readily see when the brass is ready to be soldered. When the torch flame is at its maximum heating point, apply to the butted ends of the brass. Count slowly to 60 or 70; hold torch steadily in one hand and pick up solder with the other hand. Place end of solder into the flame about 1/16″ above the red-hot brass ends. In several seconds a bubble of solder will melt and drop onto the butted ends of brass. Still keeping the flame steady on the joint, lay down the coil of solder, and pick up a small 8″ to 10″ metal file. Place end of file into the flame, but keep the main jet of the flame onto the butt. As the bubble of solder spreads out on the joint and begins to run freely, push solder with file end until it completely covers the joint. Remove torch flame from the butt and direct it slowly around the inside of the brass circle, being careful not to stop the flame at any point for this will scorch and stain the brass through to the outside. This will expand the brass circle enough so it will slip easily over the plywood circle, which should be flat on the workroom floor.

6.   Working quickly so the brass does not cool, slip on heavy leather gloves. Turn off the blow torch. Unclamp the brass rim, pick up and place one part down over any part of the plywood disc. Holding this section down with your foot, pull brass rim over and around plywood disc and push brass down around it. The rim should slip on easily, and as it cools the brass will contract and form a pressure fit around the plywood.

If you were not able to get the brass rim on, reheat and try again. If the butt joint has loosened, cut a small strip off the end with the tin snips and repeat the process. This process can be used for pressure fitting on round, oval or outgoing free forms.

7. File off the excess solder and any scorch marks at the point of the braze with a file used for metal until it is completely clean. Sand around the outside of the brass rim with emery or sandpaper until it is smooth and the brazing cannot be detected. Give a satin brass finish by rubbing with steel wool. Wipe carefully with brass polish, clean and dry.

8. If the tesserae are pasted face down on paper, soak paper in warm water to loosen, then peel off. Dry the tesserae with a towel. Keep in separate piles by color.

9. Adjust depth of plywood from top of brass rim. Lay a thick tessera along inside of brass edging. Adjust brass rim so that its top is even with or very slightly above surface of the tesserae. Push rim into position, or turn the table top over and tap plywood lightly with a hammer until the adjustment is correct.

10. Completely cover brass edging with masking tape.

11. Put a thin ribbon of mosaic adhesive around the inside edge where the brass edging meets the plywood. Let adhesive dry.

12. Place kraft paper over the top, and draw a circle just inside the brass rim. Cut out paper circle and place it on the table top. It should fit the table top exactly, and barely miss touching the rim.

13. Squeeze a 6″ ribbon of Duco cement along outside edge of kraft paper circle. Place black tesserae smooth side down, beveled ridged side up, into the cement, with leading edges (the edge of the tessera away from the rim) meeting or next to each other. The tesserae are not always exactly square; matching the leading edges ensures more even circles as you work in toward the center. If you push the tesserae in the first row to the rim, and succeeding rows toward the rim, instead of matching the leading edges, the second and succeeding rows will be increasingly uneven and the design will lose its symmetrical effect. Repeat the cementing and placement of black tesserae until the outside circle is completed. Cut a few black tesserae into halves and substitute a half about every 9″ to 12″ to break the monotony of the whole tesserae. You will notice that black and some other colors are more difficult to cut than some other colors.

14. In cutting the tesserae, hold the cutter toward the ends of the handle to get better leverage. Hold a tessera on one edge between thumb and forefinger. Place opposite edge of tessera 1/16″ to ⅛″ into the edge of the cutter; give a sharp snip to fracture straight across into two even halves. To make smaller pieces, place halves into cutter and cut again. This is easier than trying to cut smaller pieces from the whole ¾″ square tessera.

15. When the row is filled in, start new row just inside it, repeating process. Align the leading edges to keep symmetry of your design. Repeat rows. A sunburst design is most beautiful when the transition of color is gradual and subtle, a "weaving" from the darker to lighter shades as it nears the center. As you place row after row, gradually work in the lighter shades so that some of the darker shades overlap into the rows of lighter shade, and vice versa. If you have been too abrupt in the color transition, pull off some of the tesserae in the rows already laid, spread more cement, and place tesserae of different shadings.

As you get in toward the middle fill in the rows almost completely with half and shortened tesserae; this enhances the design and also gives less space between the pieces at the edge opposite the leading inside edge. Use shortened tesserae in the last two full rows in the center. Shorten tesserae by cutting in half, then cutting ⅛″ to ¼″ off one long end. Shortened tesserae should be the same length within a row, and gradual by rows; two or three rows out from the center the tesserae will not be shortened as much as for the rows closer to the center.

For the centerpiece, chip the edges of a full ¾″ tessera until it is round; fit into center. You may have to cut several pieces before you get one properly rounded for the center.

16. Check overall effect. Remove any tesserae that do not seem to blend into the color gradation and replace with more suitable pieces.

17. Lift out wrapping paper with the tesserae, and place on a flat surface.

18. Apply a thin brush coat of shellac to the plywood top. Let dry.

19. Put the cement in mixing bowl. To prepare tint (so cement will blend in with black and gray tesserae), put 1 or 2 level teaspoons of black mineral pigment into a water glass, mix in enough water to make a paste, then add water until three fourths full. Stir vigorously with a teaspoon. When the dye is in a temporary state of evenness throughout the water, pour mixture down side of bowl. Work the dye solution into the cement with a tablespoon or with your hand (your hand does a better mixing job). Add water, pouring it down side of bowl a little at a time while stirring slowly. Mix until dye is evenly worked in, and the cement is smooth and the consistency of *very very* thick pancake batter. If you have added too much water, add more cement until it is the right consistency. Cover bowl with a damp cloth while applying mosaic adhesive to the table top.

20.   Squeeze the five-ounce tube of mosaic adhesive onto the table top. Spread evenly over the entire surface with a piece of cardboard or flat-edged wood. If more is needed, use the two-ounce tube also. Be careful to keep adhesive from getting on the hands; it will hamper you in spreading the cement. It is difficult to remove from the hands, but lighter fluid will take it off.

21.   Check masking tape to make sure it is still completely covering the brass edging to protect it from the cement.

22.   If cement has dried slightly and seems difficult to work with, add a drop of water and work it with your hands until the proper consistency. Pour cement over the wet adhesive on the table top. Spread evenly over the surface with your hand, being careful not to spread so thin your hand touches the wet adhesive.

23.   Lift the entire sheet of paper with the tesserae glued to it, turn and place mosaic down into the cement (you will probably need help with this). If any tesserae fall off into the cement before the mosaic is in place, lift out and lay aside, with any others that may fall out in the turning; these can be placed later. If paper does not fit evenly within the rim or part of the mosaic is not within the rim at some point, push top of paper around slightly with your hand until it fits snugly within the rim.

24.   Place the flat of your hand in the center of the paper, and with slight pressure, move your hand in a circular motion in larger and larger circles until you reach the edge. Any excess cement under the mosaic will be forced out and over the rim. Repeat for a few minutes until the paper is relatively flat, and the paper and tesserae are flush with the top of the brass rim.

25.   Dampen the paper, using a sponge and a little water. Let it soak for 3 to 5 minutes. Push rolling pin over the paper to loosen the Duco. Insert fingernail under dampened paper and work up a strip along the edge for several inches. Then peel paper off in strips, working toward center, until paper is removed and the mosaic is "floating" freely in the wet cement. With fingernail or a razor blade, remove any small pieces of paper still sticking to the tesserae.

26.   Replace any pieces that fell off the paper when turning and placing the mosaic into the cement. Run hand gently over top of the mosaic in a circular motion until the tesserae form symmetrical circles. If an occasional tessera has been pushed under another one, move the ad-

joining one aside a bit with a circular motion of the hand, and push
the trapped piece back into place. If a tessera is high or raised above
the surrounding area, and one in an adjoining area seems lower,
place a flat object on the areas. The cement
will be oozed from under the high piece to
beneath the low piece.

Run a rolling pin over the entire top vigorously until the cement has oozed up level
with the tops of the tesserae, and the surface is perfectly smooth.

The laying of the mosaic in the cement is easier if done quickly before the cement sets, hardens, and becomes difficult to work with
(usually about one hour). Should this happen, add a small amount of
water and work cement where you need to re-lay pieces. Let cement
set for about a half hour.

27.   Wipe the surface gently with a dampened cloth or sponge to remove any cement from the top of the tesserae. Do not try to clean
thoroughly at this time; you may push some of the pieces out of place,
or make the top uneven.

28.   Examine the top carefully, removing with a toothpick any bits of
paper or dried adhesive stuck between the tesserae, before the cement
dries. Fill in any little holes you have made with the toothpick, with
some of the leftover cement. If it has dried, dip a lump of it into water,
then work it in your hand until it becomes sticky and malleable. Gently
rub this into the holes with a circular motion. Let dry for a minute, then
wipe off excess with a slightly damp cloth. Let cement dry 8 to 12
hours.

29.   Sponge off the top with clear water. If the chalky film of cement
does not come off the mosaic easily, wet surface and scrub vigorously
with copper scouring pads; scrape with penknife if necessary. When
clean, wipe the surface with a dry cloth. Let dry for a time, then wipe
again with a damp cloth. The top should be clean. Let it dry for several hours.

30.   When the top is completely dry, waterproof the cement between
the tesserae with silicone marble polish. Shake bottle of polish vigorously, pour a few ounces onto the mosaic and spread with a cloth. Let
it soak into the cement for thirty minutes. Wipe with a cloth, then
polish the surface. Waterproofing the cement in this way prevents staining; the tesserae, of course, are stainproof.

31.   Turn table top over and stain the bottom with a wood stain, pouring a small amount onto the plywood and spreading it over the entire
surface with a lint-free cloth. Rub the stain over the surface evenly,
then wipe off any excess. Let it dry.

32.   Mark underside for placement of leg flanges. Place a pencil dot in the exact center. Divide into three even pie-shaped sections, drawing lines from the center to the rim. Measure in 4″ from the rim, at the three lines along the edge. Place the flanges on the lines, with the outer edges in 4″ from the rim, as marked. Mark through with a pencil for the screw holes. Remove flanges. With hammer and nail, or an electric drill, make small holes at the pencil points. Place flanges over holes, one flange at a time, and attach with ¾″ round head steel wood screws. Start screws with a light tap of a hammer, then screw flanges down firmly. Tap the plastic leg tips onto the hollow ends of the metal legs with a hammer. Screw legs tightly into the flanges.

33.   Turn table right side up and peel masking tape from edging. Coat brass with clear lacquer. If the lacquer coating on the legs is very thin, give another coat to prevent tarnishing. The lacquer will dry more evenly and quickly if applied on a dry, nonhumid day.

Book Ends

These hardwood book ends with a butterfly design in Italian tesserae, using the direct method of application, will add interest and beauty to any room.

Equipment and Supplies

1. A pair of hardwood (mahogany, walnut or other hardwood) triangular book ends that measure 5"x5"x7" on the triangle side, with the base and back each measuring 5" square. If book ends of this type and size are not available, purchase a 5" square block of hardwood, and have it cut diagonally through to make two triangular blocks of the above size.
2. Matching wood edging ¼" square: 4 strips 7" long, and 4 strips 4½" long.
3. Italian glass tesserae ¾" square: 10 orange, 8 dark blue, 8 turquoise, 20 white, 15 light gray, 2 dark green, 2 light blue, 6 yellow, 4 black.
4. Five-ounce tube of mosaic adhesive.
5. One-half to one pound mosaic cement.
6. Mosaic cutter.
7. Small finishing nails.
8. Sandpaper.
9. Carpenter's glue.
10. Shellac and brush.
11. Wood file.
12. Masking tape 1" wide.
13. Mixing bowl and cloth.
14. Linseed or tung oil; furniture wax.

Instructions

1. If book ends were cut from a square block of hardwood for you, sand the cut surface.
2. Glue the 7" edging strips along the long edge of the diagonal surface. Glue the 4½" strips at ends of the 7" strips, fitting corners evenly. A good wood glue, such as Elmer's, will hold the strips adequately, but

small finishing nails may be used if necessary. Let glue set so it will hold the edging.

3. Smooth corners of edging with wood file, then with sandpaper.

4. Cover top and outside of edging and the back surfaces with masking tape.

5. Apply a thin brush coat of shellac to the flat diagonal surface inside the edging, to prevent the adhesive from soaking into the wood.

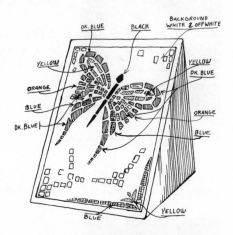

6. With a soft lead pencil draw a line from the upper right corner to the bottom left corner to indicate the *approximate* angle of the butterfly design. Following the diagram, roughly sketch butterfly onto the wood. Indicate approximate areas where the colored tesserae are to be placed.

7. Separate and spread out tesserae by color.

8. Part of the butterfly design and background requires smaller cut pieces of tesserae. Following the diagram, cut the pieces of a single color needed as you fill in the butterfly outline, starting with the orange. To cut tesserae hold cutter near the handle end for better leverage. Hold the tessera by one edge between thumb and forefinger. Place the opposite edge of tessera 1/16" to ⅛" inside the cutter. Close cutter until it holds the tessera directly in the middle and forming a right angle, cutter edge to tessera edge. Place left hand over right hand holding the cutter, straighten left arm for addi-

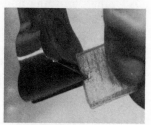

tional leverage, and snip sharply. The tessera should fracture straight across, giving you two even halves. Cut several more pieces in half. Now cut these halves into small thin pieces until you have a dozen or so. Most of the orange pieces should be long and thin since they form the major outline of the butterfly. In cutting the small pieces it is best to first cut a tessera in half, and from the half piece cut smaller ones, when doing small chipped mosaic work such as this.

9. Squeeze a small ribbon of mosaic adhesive over the area to be filled in with the long thin orange chips. Wait 3 to 5 minutes until the adhesive becomes tacky, then fill in the orange pieces. If the small thin pieces are placed on the book end while the adhesive is still very wet, they may fall off. Cut pieces of another color, apply the mosaic adhesive, and fill in, following the design. Continue until the butterfly is completely filled in. Use a toothpick to push the smaller pieces into place to avoid touching and moving pieces already placed in the design.

10. The background, except for a strip of turquoise along the lower right side, is primarily made up of very small squares of white, and shadings of light gray. Following the photograph of the completed book end, outline with pencil the turquoise strip and light gray areas. Continuing the procedure of cutting, applying adhesive, and placing the pieces of tesserae, fill in the turquoise section, the gray shaded areas, and finally fill in the white pieces.

11. Change any pieces which do not seem to fit into the design. Apply lighter fluid to the spots, pry up the pieces, and fill in with pieces more appropriately shaped. Let adhesive dry 20 to 48 hours.

12. Test to see how well the adhesive is holding the chips by running your hand over the surface. Loose pieces should be re-glued with additional adhesive. All chips should be held firmly in place when the cement is added to the mosaic.

13. Put about one half pound of cement into a bowl. Add water, pouring it down side of the bowl a little at a time while stirring slowly with a spoon or with your hand. Mix until cement is smooth and the consistency of very heavy pancake batter.

14. Pour some of the mixed cement over the mosaic and spread with your hand, working it into the cracks. Add more cement if necessary, and rub until all the spaces are filled. Let stand 3 to 5 minutes to permit cement to settle. Wipe excess cement from surface with your hand or a dry cloth, being careful not to scoop cement from between the chips. Do not try to clean thoroughly at this time. Let stand 15 to 20 minutes.

15. With a slightly damp cloth wipe surface again so that it is clean of all cement, except for a chalky film. Let dry 4 to 10 hours.

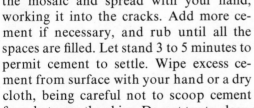

16. Sponge off the chalky film. If it does not come off easily, wet surface and scrub vigorously with copper scouring pads. When clean, dry the surface. Let stand 15 to 30 minutes.

17. To waterproof the cement between the tesserae, rub with a small amount of silicone marble polish.

18. Remove masking tape. Smooth the wood with sandpaper. Remove all wood dust. Finish with linseed oil, tung oil, or furniture wax. Repeat application over several days, then repeat once a week for two or three weeks, to give the book ends a nice finish. If, after finishing, the wood seems a bit rough, rub with very fine steel wool until smooth, and reapply oil or wax.

Oval Sunburst Coffee Table

The shadings in the Pelv Italian tesserae, applied by the indirect method, make a beautiful and subtle transition in this sunburst design. The thin tapered natural finish slanting legs and matching edging give this 24"x28" oval coffee table a light floating quality. This is truly a decorator table worth five or six times the amount it costs to make yourself.

Equipment and Supplies

1. An oval of ¾" thick exterior grade plywood, 48"x24".
2. A strip of walnut edging ⅛" thick, 1"x15'.
3. Four 15" tapered walnut wood legs.
4. Four slant flanges.
5. Sixteen ¾" round head steel wood screws.
6. Finishing nails.
7. Saw, wood clamps, screw driver.
8. Sandpaper.
9. Carpenter's glue.
10. Plastic wood, walnut color; and wood stain, walnut finish.
11. Clear shellac and brush.
12. Tung or linseed oil, and furniture wax.
13. Masking tape, 1" wide.
14. Pelv Italian tesserae: 2½ sq. ft. No. 115B, deep lavender; 2½ sq. ft. No. 114B, dark lavender; 1¼ sq. ft. No. 112A, lavender; ¾ sq. ft. No. 110A, light lavender.
15. One five-ounce and one two-ounce tube of mosaic adhesive.
16. Seven to eight pounds of mosaic cement.
17. Small amount of Venetian Red mineral pigment.
18. Mosaic cutter.
19. Two tubes of Duco cement.

20. A square of kraft wrapping paper 26"x50".
21. Two copper scouring pads.
22. Large mixing bowl, rolling pin, cloths, string.
23. Silicone marble polish.

Instructions

1. If the plywood is not cut in an oval, shape your own from a 48"x24" rectangle. To shape the oval, measure and mark center of each edge of the rectangle 12" from corner on 24" ends; drive nails in lightly at these marks. Tie string to nails, tightly for a "thin" oval, loosely for a "fat" oval. Place pencil at the mid-point of the string on one side and push string out toward edge of the plywood. If string is adjusted correctly when pencil pushes it out to 12" from center of plywood, a perfect oval will result. Trace string outline onto plywood with pencil by pushing along string and using it as a guide. Saw along outline. Sandpaper edge.

2. Have your carpenter put on the walnut edging flush with bottom of plywood and approximately ¼" higher than plywood top surface. If he uses more than one strip of edging make certain the strips match in grain and color, and that he makes a careful seam. If you are a home carpenter you may perform this difficult task yourself. Place plywood oval flat on a working surface. Heat the edging with steam or very hot water, and pull it carefully around the edge of the plywood, applying a good carpenter's glue, and then clamping the edging. A few very small finishing nails may be countersunk into the edging at intervals and near the joint. Fill in nail holes with plastic wood or walnut-colored putty. Let glue dry 8 to 12 hours until edging is firmly held to the plywood. Finish off edging with careful sanding.

3. Cover the edging with masking tape. Apply a thin brush coat of shellac to both top and bottom of plywood. This prevents water in the cement from soaking into the dry wood, and weakening the cement and warping the plywood. Let dry.

4. Soak tesserae in warm water 10 to 20 minutes to loosen backing paper. Peel off the paper. Dry tesserae with a towel. Separate into piles by color shades.

5. When the shellac has dried, place sheet of kraft wrapping paper on oval surface. Trace outline of oval top and cut out. The paper oval should fit exactly the table top, and barely miss touching the edging. Place paper oval on table top.

6. Squeeze a 6" ribbon of Duco cement along edge of oval. Using the darkest lavender tesserae, place one, smooth side down, beveled ridged side up, into the adhesive. Continue placing them into the Duco, leading edges (the edge of the tessera opposite the edge along table rim) meeting. This ensures even ovals as you work succeeding rows in toward the center. Repeat the cement and placement of tesserae until the oval is completed. Cut some of the tesserae into halves and use to fill in spaces along rim edge of table where tesserae edges are farther apart at the ends (because they meet at the leading edges); and to break the monotony of the pattern.

7. In cutting the tesserae, hold the cutter toward the ends of the handle to get better leverage. Hold a tessera on one edge between thumb and forefinger. Place opposite edge of tessera 1/16″ to ⅛″ into the edge of the cutter; give a sharp snip. To make smaller pieces, place halves into cutter and cut again.

8. When outside row is filled in, start next row just inside it, repeating process of outer row. Align leading edges to keep symmetry of design. Repeat rows.

A sunburst design is most beautiful when the transition of color is gradual and subtle, a "weaving" from the darker to lighter shades as it nears the center. As you place row after row, gradually work in the lighter shades so that some of the darker shades overlap into the rows of lighter shade, and vice versa. If you have been too abrupt in the color transition, pull off some of the tesserae in the rows you have laid, spread more Duco, and place tesserae of different shadings. The last several rows and the center will be filled in almost completely with half tesserae and shortened tesserae. Shorten tesserae by cutting in half, then cutting ⅛″ to ¼″ off one long end. Shortened tesserae should be the same length within a row, and gradual by rows, as you work in toward the center.

9. Fill in the center with shortened pieces, with triangular pieces at the ends of center oval, and quarter pieces toward the center. Cut triangular pieces by placing tessera into cutter at an angle.

10. Check overall design effect. Remove any that do not blend into the color gradation and replace, until pleased with the shading.

11. Lift out wrapping paper with the tesserae, and place on a flat surface.

12. Put another thin coat of shellac on table top. Let dry.

13. Put the dry cement in a bowl. To prepare tint (so cement will blend in with lavender tesserae), put 3 to 4 level teaspoons of Venetian Red mineral pigment into a water glass, mix in enough water to make a paste, then add water until glass is three fourths full. Stir vigorously with a teaspoon. When the dye is in a temporary state of evenness throughout the water, pour mixture gradually down side of bowl. Work the dye solution into the cement with a tablespoon or with your hand (your hand does a better mixing job). Add water, pouring it down side of bowl a little at a time while stirring slowly. Mix until dye is evenly worked in, and the cement is smooth and the consistency of *very very* thick pancake batter. Add more cement if it is not thick enough. Cover bowl with a damp cloth while applying mosaic adhesive to table top.

14. Squeeze the five-ounce tube of mosaic adhesive onto the table top. Spread evenly over entire surface with a piece of cardboard or flat-edged wood. If more is needed, use the two-ounce tube also. Keep adhesive from getting on the hands; it will hamper you in spreading the cement. It is difficult to remove from the hands, but lighter fluid will take it off.

15. Check masking tape to make sure it is still completely covering the edging to protect it from the cement.

16. If cement has dried slightly and seems difficult to work with, add a drop of water and work it with your hands until the proper consistency. Pour cement over the wet adhesive on the table top. Spread evenly over surface, carefully so your hand does not touch the wet adhesive beneath the cement.

17. Lift the entire sheeet of paper with the tesserae glued to it, turn and place mosaic down into the cement (you will probably need help with this). If any tesserae fall off into the cement before the mosaic is in place, lift out and lay aside, with any others that may fall out in the turning; these can be placed later. If paper does not fit evenly within the rim or part of the mosaic is not within the rim at some point, push top of paper around slightly with your hand until it fits snugly within the rim.

18. Place the flat of your hand in the center of the paper, and with slight pressure, move your hand in a circular motion in larger and larger circles until you reach the edge. Any excess cement under the mosaic will be forced out and over the edging. Repeat for a few minutes until the paper is relatively flat, and the paper and tesserae are flush with the top of the edging.

19. Dampen the paper, using a sponge and a little water. Let it soak for 3 to 5 minutes. Insert fingernail under dampened paper and work up a strip along the edge for several inches. Then peel paper off in strips, working toward center, until paper is removed and the mosaic is "floating" freely in the wet cement. Pick with fingernail or a razor blade any small pieces of paper still sticking to tesserae.

20. Replace any pieces that fell off the paper when turning and placing the tesserae into the cement. Run hand gently over top of the mosaic in a circular motion until the tesserae form symmetrical rows. If an occasional piece has been pushed under another one, move the adjoining one aside a bit with a circular motion of the hand, and push the trapped piece back into place. If a tessera is high or raised above the surrounding area, and one in an adjoining area seems lower, place a flat object on the areas. The cement in the area will be oozed from the high and under the low tessera, pushing the high piece down and raising the low piece. Contrary to popular belief tesserae do not sink down into the cement unless the cement is very thin.

Run a rolling pin over the entire top vigorously and with enough pressure so that the cement will ooze up level with the tops of the tesserae, making the surface perfectly smooth.

The laying of the mosaic in the cement is easier done quickly before the cement sets, hardens, and is difficult to work with (usually about one hour). Should it become too hard, add a small amount of water and work cement where you need to re-lay tesserae. Let cement set for about a half hour.

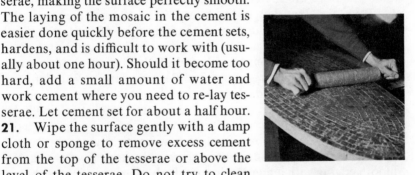

21. Wipe the surface gently with a damp cloth or sponge to remove excess cement from the top of the tesserae or above the level of the tesserae. Do not try to clean thoroughly at this time; you may push some of the pieces out of place, or make the top uneven.

22. Examine the top carefully, removing with a toothpick any bits of paper or dried adhesive stuck between the tesserae, before the cement dries. Fill in any little holes you have made with the toothpick, with some of the leftover cement. If it has dried, dip a lump of it into water, then work it in your hand until it becomes sticky and malleable. Gently rub this into the holes with a circular motion. Let dry for a minute, then wipe off excess with a slightly damp cloth. Let cement dry 8 to 12 hours.

23. Sponge off the top with clear water. If the chalky film of cement does not come off the mosaic easily, wet surface and scrub vigorously with copper scouring pads; scrape with penknife if necessary. When clean, wipe the surface with a dry cloth. Let dry for a time, then wipe again with a damp cloth. The top should be clean. Let it dry for several hours.

24. When the top is completely dry, waterproof cement between the tesserae with silicone marble polish. Shake bottle of polish vigorously, pour a few ounces onto the mosaic and spread with a cloth. Let it soak into the cement for thirty minutes. Wipe with a cloth, then polish the surface. Waterproofing the cement in this way prevents staining; the tesserae, of course, are extremely rugged and stain proof.

25. Turn table top over and stain the bottom with a wood stain, pouring a small amount onto the plywood and spreading it over the entire surface with a lint-free cloth. Rub the stain over the surface evenly, then wipe off any excess. Let it dry.

26. Mark underside for placement of leg flanges. Measure from side to side and end to end, find the exact center and mark. Draw a line lengthwise to the exact center of each end. Tie a string tightly around a pencil near the point end. Hold the string, back 6″ from the pencil, onto the edge of the oval end exactly at the center line. With the pencil in the other hand, pull the 6″ string taut and draw an arc out on either side from the center line. Repeat at other end.

27. Place the slant flanges in about 3½″ to 4″ from the table edge along the arcs you have drawn on the long sides of the table. If you want the table to have a greater appearance of floating in space, place the flanges farther in from the edge. With the flanges in place, mark through with a pencil for screw holes. Remove flanges. With hammer and nail, or an electric drill, make small holes at the pencil points. Place flanges over holes, one flange at a time, and attach with ¾″ round head steel wood screws. Start screws with a light tap of a hammer, then screw flanges down firmly. Screw legs tightly into the flanges.

28. Turn table right side up and peel masking tape from the edging. Smooth edging with a fine sandpaper. Rub edging and legs with tung or linseed oil. For a fine finish, repeat oil application over several days, then repeat once or twice a week for two or three weeks. If little grains of wood become uneven, sand lightly again before an oil application. When the wood is well oiled, give it a good coating of furniture wax. Polish.

Ash Tray or Wall Hanging

A round tray 8½" in diameter covered
with mottled green and white Italian ceramic tesserae is bright and practical as
an ash tray, candy dish or wall hanging.
Made by the direct method of application.

Equipment and Supplies

1. An aluminum, steel or wooden tray 8½" in diameter, with edge
gradually curving up from center to approximately ¾" above flat bottom.
2. Seventy-six ¾" square mottled green and white Italian ceramic
tesserae.
3. Two-ounce tube of mosaic adhesive.
4. Three fourths pound of mosaic cement.
5. Mosaic cutter.
6. Scouring pads.
7. Silicone polish.
8. Mixing bowl, cloths.

Instructions

1. Wipe inside of tray to remove any dust or grease from inside surface. Place on newspaper on working surface.
2. If the tesserae are pasted face down on paper, soak paper in warm
water to loosen. After about 15 minutes peel off the paper. Dry the tesserae with a towel or cloth.
3. Squeeze a ribbon of mosaic adhesive around inside edge of the
tray, letting it ooze down the side toward the center. After several minutes the adhesive will become tacky.
4. Place a tessera into the tacky adhesive about 1/16" in from the
edge of the tray. Place a second piece next to the first with the inside, or
edge toward the center, almost touching the edge of the first tessera.
The back of the tesserae should be "square" with the outside edge of
the tray. Continue placing tesserae around the edge; this will take 28
pieces. If any move out of place, adjust them with your forefinger.
5. Squeeze another row of adhesive just inside the first row of tesserae; place 21 tesserae into this row. The third row will require 14
pieces and the fourth row, 4 tesserae.

6. Cut two tesserae into halves with a mosaic cutter. Hold the cutter toward the ends of the handle to get better leverage. Hold a tessera on one edge between thumb and forefinger. Place opposite edge of tessera 1/16″ to ⅛″ into the edge of the cutter; give a sharp snip. If the tesserae do not cut into good rectangles, snip at their edges to even. Ceramic tesserae are of a soft material and if necessary you can sandpaper the edges to smooth.

7. Squeeze adhesive into center of tray; place one tessera in the exact center. Place the four halves around the sides of the center tessera.

8. With your forefinger readjust any tesserae that have moved out of place. Let the adhesive set for 5 to 6 hours.

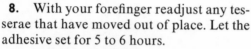
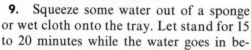

9. Squeeze some water out of a sponge or wet cloth onto the tray. Let stand for 15 to 20 minutes while the water goes in between the tesserae and is absorbed by the soft porous clay backing of the ceramic tesserae.

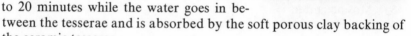

10. Place approximately ½ lb. of cement into a bowl. Add water, pouring it down side of the bowl a little at a time, and mix in with a spoon or with your hand until the mixture is the smooth consistency of pancake batter. The mixture may be of a thinner consistency for the porous ceramic tesserae than was necessary for the glass tesserae used in other projects.

11. Pour cement onto the tesserae. With your hand rub the cement over the tesserae, forcing it into the cracks between. Remove the excess cement from the surface of the tesserae with the flat of your hand, but do not scoop it from the cracks. The cement and the top surface of the tesserae should be even. Let dry for 20 to 30 minutes.

12. Go over the surface of the mosaic with a damp cloth or the flat of your hand. If the cement seems to be drying too quickly dribble a little water over the surface and clean until the cement is smooth and only a thin film of chalky cement covers the tesserae.

13. Mix the remaining cement to a heavier consistency; rub around the outside edge of the tesserae. Smooth by running your forefinger around the edge and squeezing any excess cement off onto newspaper. Let dry 1 to 2 hours.

14. Clean the top of the tesserae with a damp cloth. Smooth the cement between them. Place a damp cloth over the top and leave for 4 to 12 hours.

15. To waterproof cement, pour an ounce of silicone marble polish over the surface and let it stand for 20 to 30 minutes. Then wipe the surface with a dry cloth and polish.

16. Remove any cement from bottom of the tray; paint or polish.

Ceramic
Swimming
Pool
Table

A 36″ round table of cracked Japanese porcelain and Portuguese ceramic tesserae for either outdoor or informal living room use, it may be given fairly rough treatment. Made by the direct method, it can be assembled for less than forty dollars, one-third its finished cost.

Equipment and Supplies

1. A circle of 5-ply ¾″ thick exterior grade plywood 36″ in diameter, with the under edge beveled back at a 45° angle, filled in with plastic wood and sanded smooth.

2. Three 15″ unfinished wooden legs.

3. Three slant flanges.

4. Sixteen ¾″ No. 7 or No. 8 steel round head wood screws.

5. Clear shellac and brush.

6. White enamel and brush.

7. Screwdriver, pliers.

8. Portuguese glazed ceramic tesserae 4¼″ square: 5 sq. ft. pure white; glazed ceramic tesserae 4″ square: 2 sq. ft. light aqua blue; Japanese glazed porcelain tesserae 4″ square: ½ sq. ft. red, 1 sq. ft. black, 1 sq. ft. gold.

9. Five-ounce tube and two-ounce tube of mosaic adhesive.

10. Eight pounds of mosaic cement.

11. Mosaic cutter.

12. Mosaic or ordinary household hammer.

13. Glass cutter.

14. Leather glove.

15. Masking tape 1″ wide.

16. Scouring pads, cloths, mixing bowl.

17. Silicone marble polish.

Instructions

1.   Place the 36" round plywood on working surface and apply a coat of shellac to both top and bottom.

2.   Place the tesserae into a bucket of water; soak 1 to 3 hours.

3.   With a pencil tied to a piece of string, measure off arcs spaced approximately 4" apart, one in front of the other. Each arc becomes longer (see picture above).

4.   Pattern for filling in the arcs: first small arc, irregularly cracked ceramic and porcelain pieces of all the colors; second and third arcs, long thin cuts of white and blue ceramic tesserae; next three arcs, cover with irregularly broken ceramic and porcelain tesserae of all the colors; the last two arcs, long thin cuts of white and blue ceramic tesserae.

5.   Fill in the third, second, eighth, and seventh arcs first, in that order, with the long thin cuts of white and blue ceramic tesserae. Hold the mosaic cutter toward the ends of the handle to get better leverage. Hold a tessera on one edge between thumb and forefinger; place opposite edge ⅛" into the edge of the cutter and give a sharp snip. If they are difficult to cut, score the glazed side of the ceramic tessera with a glass cutter. Then grip one edge of the tessera with pliers, hold the opposite edge in your hand and pull down. The ceramic tessera should break evenly into long thin pieces. Do the same with some blue pieces.

6.   Using the five-ounce tube first, squeeze mosaic adhesive to cover four or five inches of the third arc, beginning at one end. Place a piece of broken white tessera, the smooth glazed side up, into the adhesive even with the bottom of the arc. Continue with the adhesive and the white and the blue strips of tesserae until the arc is filled. Break up additional pieces as needed. Check the arc for evenness of the tiles. If any need adjusting, pull up and rearrange the pieces until they form an interesting and varied pattern.

7.   Fill in the second, then the eighth, and then the seventh arcs in the same manner. Distribute the blue ceramic pieces between the white strips as indicated in the picture.

8.   Put on a leather glove to break up the tesserae into irregularly shaped pieces for the remaining arcs. Hold a tessera in the gloved hand, clay back side of piece up. Strike the middle of the tessera with a hammer to fracture it into five or more irregular pieces.

9.   Squeeze adhesive over a small area of the first arc and fit in the irregular pieces. Repeat until area is covered, then fill in the

three center arcs in the same way, contrasting and blending the colors to form an interesting pattern. If your arrangement is not
pleasing, pull up pieces that do not suit you,
and replace with others. Let the adhesive
dry 4 to 6 hours.

10.   Place masking tape around the outside edge and even with the top of the tesserae. Run forefinger around tape to make
certain it is sticking to the edge.

11.   Pour several drinking glasses of water over the top. Let it run in
between the tesserae; they are porous and will absorb it. Let stand 10 to
15 minutes, then tilt table and pour off excess water.

12.   Place approximately seven pounds of cement into a bowl. Add
water, pouring it down the side of the bowl a little at a time, and mix in
with a spoon or with your hand until the mixture is the smooth consistency of pancake batter.

13.   Pour cement onto the tesserae. With your hand spread the cement over the entire surface, pressing down to force it into the cracks
between the tesserae. Push excess cement over the edge. Let stand 5
to 10 minutes. Rub palm over the mosaic, smoothing and leveling the
top surface of the cement and tesserae.

14.   Wipe surface clean with a damp cloth, leaving a thin film of cement. Let stand approximately 1 hour.

15.   With a cloth clean the tesserae, being careful not to scoop any
of the cement from between them. Place a damp cloth over the top
and leave for 5 to 6 hours.

16.   Scrub top with scouring pads and water to remove all excess cement. Let dry ½ hour.

17.   To waterproof cement, pour about 3 ounces of silicone marble
polish over the top. Spread evenly and let it stand for ½ hour. Wipe
surface with a dry cloth, and polish.

18.   Remove masking tape from the edge.

19.   Apply a coat of white enamel paint around the outside edge of
the tesserae and the beveled back edge of the plywood base. Let dry.
Turn over and enamel the bottom side and the beveled edge again.
Let dry.

20.   Give the legs several coats of enamel.

21.   Place the three flanges evenly around the edge, in about 4″ from
the edge of the underside; screw tightly into place. Screw legs tightly
into the flanges.

PART 2: Materials and Methods

Kinds of Tesserae

The kind of tesserae, its qualities of color and strength, and its uses, is important in the choosing of material for a particular mosaic.

There are many kinds of tesserae. Almost anything that can be shaped or cut, formed into a design, and then applied to a backing, can be used to make a mosaic. However, the use and limitations of materials must be considered when you plan a mosaic. Squares of different colors of cardboard, plastic, and linoleum, for instance, have been utilized to make pleasing mosaic patterns. But a cardboard or plastic mosaic does not have the vibrancy of color, the strength, and the beauty of solid tesserae.

Tesserae may be of either the impervious, semipervious, or porous type, depending upon the internal structure of the tesserae, or how much water it will absorb over a given period of time. This is an important factor to consider in planning a particular use. It would be unwise to use a porous type for an outdoor table or bench, for moisture would soak into the tiles, freeze, and cause the tesserae to break. The type of tesserae also determines the appropriate and suitable adhesive, cement, and backing to use with it.

VENETIAN OR ITALIAN GLASS TESSERAE come usually from Venice and its environs, one of the most famous glass areas in the world. It is made from specially fired glass, mixed in a high temperature molten state with certain minerals to give it strength and color shading. The mixture is poured into small wafflelike molds. When the glass has cooled, the pieces of solid glass, colored through, are broken out of the molds and pasted face down onto paper. In the molding it attains a slight bevel along the sides and slight ridges on the underside. The ridges aid in adhering the mosaic to backings and surfaces.

These tesserae come in about 100 colors arranged by color families. For example, about 10 shadings in the aqua blue family, ranging from a very deep aqua to an almost white aqua, insure magnificent color gradation.

Ordinarily the Italian glass tesserae come in ¾″ squares. Other sizes are manufactured, but rarely imported to the U.S. They come pasted face down (the smooth surface) on one-foot-square sheets of paper. Each sheet holds 225 tesserae of the same color. When ready to use, the sheet is placed in warm water to loosen the tesserae; they are then peeled from the paper.

Prices vary by color, usually starting at about $2 a square foot for light shades. Reds, oranges, yellows, and golds are the most expensive, usually from $7 to $10 a sheet. Sizable discounts can usually be obtained on quantity purchases of 30 or more sheets of a single color.

Sample cuts, color chart, and foot square sheet
of Italian glass tesserae.

Italian glass tesserae is an economical all-purpose material that can be used on floors, sidewalks, walls, tables, and fireplace fronts, as well as in small art objects. It does not deteriorate with age like marble or porous materials. Once embedded in cement, it is almost indestructible. It is impervious, so will not stain; and since it is almost smooth, dirt does not hold to it readily. With the exception of several colors, it is of uniform thickness; making it excellent for smooth table and counter tops.

Trivets (left) made with Italian glass tesserae. Lamp base (right) by
Jack Kidder and James Dorris, made with small cuts
of Italian glass tesserae.

It is slightly translucent, so it can be used like stained glass; this method is called *Mosaialight,* a Mosaic Crafts invention (patent pending).

Italian glass tesserae are used in Projects 1, 3, 4, 6, 7, 8, 9, and 10.

GLAZED CERAMIC AND PORCELAIN TILES. Ceramic tile is made of clay with a thin vitreous glaze on the top surface. Once embedded in a proper cement it is quite strong. Depending upon the thickness of the glaze and the strength of the clay backing, it can be used in much the same way as the Italian tesserae.

Ceramic tile is usually quite porous and not suited for outdoor use, where moisture would soak into the tiles, freeze, and cause the tiles to break, or for floors, where heavy use would scratch the glaze.

It gives more of a surface shine or glare than the Italian tesserae, and does not have the delicacy of color gradations. The solid colors do not mix as effectively as the Italian glass. It comes in a range of 30 to 50 solid colors, and also in mottled shadings, such as black with green spots, or in plaids of different colors. In objects where color gradation is not important, and variation is desired, a mottled ceramic tile is effective. While useful for table tops, counter surfaces, and walls, it does not impart the pleasing color sense of the Italian; nor is it generally as strong.

Game table with leather edging (left) made with hand-fired glazed ceramic tesserae by the direct method. Oval coffee table (right) by Jack Gregory; outside rows made of cuts of Spanish glazed ceramic tesserae, center of cuts of hand-fired glazed ceramic tesserae, by the direct method.

Made in Italy, Puerto Rico, Japan, the U.S., and other countries, ceramic tiles are ¾" square and usually come pasted face down on one-foot-square sheets of paper. Each sheet holds 225 tiles of the same color. When ready to use, the sheet is placed in warm water to loosen the tiles; they are then peeled from the paper. Prices range upward from about $2 a sheet.

The Japanese porcelain tile has a thick vitreous glaze and is semi-impervious. It is a stronger tile than ceramic and has wider use; for instance, it may be used outdoors in freezing climates. It comes in a variety of sizes from smaller than the ¾" square to 2" squares and larger.

Ceramic and porcelain tiles may be cut and shaped with mosaic cutters in the same way that Italian tesserae are cut. Rough edges of the soft clay-backed tiles can be smoothed with sandpaper; emery paper is necessary for the harder porcelain and Italian tesserae. These latter rarely need smoothing for the glaze usually cuts without chipping.

These ceramic tiles ordinarily do not have a bevel on the back, but are sometimes slightly grooved. Their porous backs require different cementing procedures from porcelain and glass, so that they do not absorb too much water from the cement. This is discussed in the sections on application methods.

These tesserae are used in Project 12.

UNGLAZED CERAMIC AND PORCELAIN TILES. Unglazed is a term used to describe a nonshiny, dull glaze or matte finish ceramic or porcelain tile. The unglazed ceramic tiles are porous, even the top glaze to a slight extent.

It is usually made up by individual ceramists for special effects, is made in various sizes, and prices vary considerably. A few companies in this country and in Europe make a matte finish tile, but it is not readily available. Bathroom tile contractors and mosaic stores sometimes stock this type of tile, usually in large 6" to 8" squares, and the color range is limited.

The unglazed porcelain tile is colored through, and comes in various shapes and sizes. This is a bathroom floor type tile, and a fair range of dull pastel shades are available through mosaic stores. It is quite strong, but can be cut in the same way as the Italian glass and ceramic tiles. It does not have the vibrancy or range of color of the Italian and Byzantine tesserae; however, with a careful blending of color and judicious cutting, this tile can be used to create subtle effects.

BYZANTINE TESSERAE. The Italian glass tesserae is the most practical and economical for most mosaic work, but Byzantine is regarded as the king of mosaics. Most of the breath-taking mosaic murals in Ravenna, Italy, were made with it. The most exquisite nuance of shading can be achieved with Byzantine; over 7,000 shades are made.

It is manufactured in small family operated glass shops on the Island of Murano, Venice, Italy. It is made from the famous Murano glass, which is melted then poured onto a flat surface to form colorful ⅜" thick circles. When the glass has cooled, it is scored into nar-

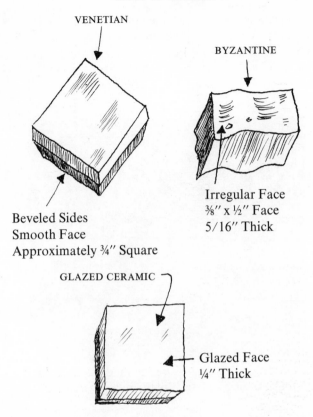

VENETIAN

BYZANTINE

Beveled Sides
Smooth Face
Approximately ¾″ Square

Irregular Face
⅜″ x ½″ Face
5/16″ Thick

GLAZED CERAMIC

Glazed Face
¼″ Thick

row irregular lines, then broken into tiny rectangles. The scored side has brilliant color refractions, often with minute air bubbles, and is usually the surface exposed in setting a mosaic piece.

Byzantine is a solid tessera, strong, impervious, and can be used in murals, walls, floors, and all furniture. If a smooth surface is desired with Byzantine, the reverse or indirect method of application, discussed in a later section, is necessary. A marble grinding wheel and water can be used on Byzantine to achieve the fine smoothness of marble.

In Italy the Byzantine tesserae are cut and shaped by the use of a small pointed hammer, or by striking with a mallet down onto a pointed chisel-shaped form. This method is slow and not very accurate; the mosaic cutters used for Italian glass and ceramic tesserae are efficiently quick and accurate.

Byzantine is not readily available in this country, but several of the larger mosaic stores are now stocking up to 125 colors. Almost any color can be obtained with a wait of 10 to 12 weeks. It is sold in bulk at about $2.50 a pound for light shades, with bright colors costing more. Two and one half pounds are needed to cover a surface one foot square. It is used in Project 5.

MARBLE TESSERAE is made of marble cut into cubes slightly less than ½″ square. It has a subtle beauty, and the colors, while limited, are quite effective. It lacks the vibrancy of color of the Italian glass, Byzantine, and ceramic tesserae, but its natural stone quality compensates in many ways.

End table top with brass edge made with Italian
marble cube tesserae, by the indirect method.

The natural marble colors range from Carrara, which is white, through Yellow Siennas, Belgium Black, Bardiglio Grey, Rosa Corallo, Botticino Beige, pinks, greens, and others. It is usually unpolished. After the mosaic piece is completed, the color is highlighted by the application of oils. It can be cut into various shapes with a mosaic cutter or a sharpened chisel, but without great accuracy. Almost all marble tesserae comes from Italy.

It is not readily available in the U.S., but nine colors are obtainable in some of the larger mosaic supply outlets. Prices range from 60¢ to $1 a pound; it takes 4 to 5 pounds to cover a foot square surface.

STAINED GLASS can be used as tesserae for mosaic pieces. Varieties include clear, uneven with air bubbles, streaked with different colors, and many others. It is produced in the U.S. and many European countries.

It can be cut by scoring with a glass cutter, or broken with a mosaic cutter. A leather glove should be worn to prevent injury, and sharp edges should be ground down with a pumice or emery stone. Once adhered to a base and cemented it is fairly strong.

It is ordinarily sold by the square foot, but breakage pieces can also be purchased for 60¢ to 80¢ a pound, at larger mosaic dealers, or from local stained glass contractors.

Coffee table top or wall hanging by Donald Schenker, made with cuts of stained glass over silver foil, by the direct method.

BOTTLE GLASS that is colored, and broken into shapes, can be used for murals and furniture. The glass is cut into smaller pieces with a mosaic cutter. After the pieces are cut, the sharp edges should be filed down.

SHELLS. Oyster, clam, and other beach shells, selected for color value, can be used in some mosaic pieces effectively. If carefully embedded in cement they will be fairly strong. Color can be increased by wetting with an oily substance after the mosaic is completed.

BEACH STONES AND PEBBLES that are colorful can be used. To retain the color after the stones are set in cement, apply oil or shellac.

COLORED SAND can be added to wet cement after it has been poured. Smoothed down, it creates interesting backgrounds for mosaic murals.

MOSAIC CANES are small rods of multicolored glass. They are manufactured in Italy in the vicinity of Venice. Small round pieces can be broken off with a mosaic cutter and used with other types of tesserae for bright accents or as ribbons for outlining.

PALLADIANO is basically the same material as Italian glass tesserae, and with the same strength and beauty. Made in sheets, like window glass, rather than in small squares, it can be broken into various shapes with a rubber-tipped hammer, and then cut into smaller pieces with a mosaic cutter. It is usually sold broken, and by the pound.

All of the foregoing types of tesserae can be used individually, in combinations, or mixed to make a mosaic piece. Choice will depend upon the purpose, effect, and style desired by the mosaic craftsman.

While the last mentioned types—shells, stones, bottle glass, and the like—can be used by themselves for mosaic pieces, for most practical purposes they should be combined with the more efficient and colorful tesserae, such as Byzantine, Italian, and ceramic. Mixing of various types of materials, known as a collage, is technically not difficult, but it is often difficult to attain a fine effect. Generally, it is recommended that the beginner confine himself to Italian or Byzantine tesserae for murals, and to Italian glass or ceramic tesserae, using the direct method of application if for furniture.

Although the finest and most usable tesserae come from Italy, it is interesting to note that they are rarely used there in furniture, their use being confined to murals, building fronts, and sidewalks. The use of tesserae for tables, book ends, trays, counter tops, and the like was started primarily by Americans.

CHAPTER 2

Cutting and Shaping Tesserae

Tesserae can be cut and shaped in various ways—with tile cut nippers (which we refer to as mosaic cutters), diamond or carborundum wheels, rubber mallet and steel chisels, glass cutters, or by striking with a hammer.

TILE CUT NIPPERS (MOSAIC CUTTERS) are the most accurate; they are also fast and clean cutting. They can be purchased at most mosaic and many hardware stores. Among the cutters that will give satisfactory service are Channelock No. 356, Dunlap, Wall Tile Nippers, Starrett No. 1, and Red Devil. The cost of these vary from $1.50 to $11.50, with the Starrett the most expensive. It is a machine-action cutter, cuts accurately, can be adjusted for the varying thicknesses of tesserae, and is easy on the hand. If you anticipate doing a considerable amount of mosaic work involving cutting, it is a good purchase. Whatever cutter is used, it should have the pincers coming together in a straight line to each other.

Various kinds of mosaic cutters.

The basic cutting technique is the same for all types of tesserae:

1. Hold the tessera to be cut between the thumb and the side of the forefinger, with the thumb on top for a firm grip.

2. In the other hand, hold the cutter far back on the handles. Hook the thumb around the top handle; manipulate the bottom handle with the other fingers.

3. Open the cutter and place the cutting edges 1/16" to ⅛" over the edge of the tessera away from the hand holding the tessera. The cutter edges will be at a right angle to the tessera edge, and directly in its middle. Grip the tessera firmly within the cutter edges by squeezing the handles of the cutter.

4. Give a sharp snip and the tessera will break, leaving the two pieces still held firmly between the thumb and forefinger. These two pieces can then be cut to form smaller pieces.

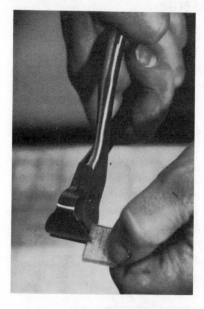

Placing tesserae into cutter (left), and (right) tesserae after cutting.

Tesserae can be cut in any size and shape. When the cutter is used correctly a fracture line is formed in the exact direction the cutter edge is aimed. It is not necessary to place the tessera completely inside the cutter; it will be difficult to cut, and will probably shatter instead of fracturing.

Smoothing the edges of cut tesserae is not usually necessary, nor is it esthetically desirable with the impervious types, unless a very even quality is desired. In this case, file smooth by placing the tessera edge against the side of a fine grain grinding wheel, or by rubbing the cut edge against a sand stone or carborundum block.

If in cutting porous types of tesserae—ceramic and porcelain—the top glaze sometimes breaks and shows the under clay aggregate, the smoothing is best done with a grinding wheel.

Mosaic cutters are used in Projects 3, 8, 9, 10, 11, and 12.

DIAMOND OR CARBORUNDUM WHEELS will cut Italian and ceramic tesserae into small and various shaped pieces. A 4″ diamond wheel, costing from $10 to $40, can be mounted onto the shaft of an electrical motor. A small platform with a notch cut in it to allow for the tip of the diamond wheel can be mounted above and slightly to the side of the motor. The cutting edge of the diamond wheel should not be more than 3/16″ above the surface of the platform. Arrange a jet of water or coolent fluid so that a thin spray will hit where the tessera contacts the cutting wheel. Arrange a guard protector to prevent flying pieces from striking you.

A carborundum wheel of this size costs about $1, but it will not last as long or make as good a cut as a diamond wheel.

CHISEL AND MALLET, the ancient and European method of breaking tesserae into different shapes, is used in various ways.

Place the tessera on a flat surface, preferably inside a box so the sides will prevent pieces from flying about. Hold a chisel against the tessera, ⅛″ to ½″ in from its edge. Aim the chisel in the direction of the desired cut. With a hammer, strike the end of the chisel with a light sharp blow.

Or mount a coal chisel in a vise with the cutting edge up. Hold the tesserae between thumb and forefinger, place its edge over the chisel about ⅛″, and strike with a sharp blow of a hard rubber mallet or a lighter blow with a steel-head hammer. The tessera should fracture nicely. A steel-head hammer is used in Project 12.

In the third method a tile cutter's hammer is used. A lightweight efficient and inexpensive one is the Dasco No. 377, costing less than $2. It and other tile cutter hammers can be purchased at hardware or some mosaic stores. Hold the tessera flat by one edge with your thumb. Grip the tile hammer in your other hand, and with its pointed head strike the edge of the tessera away from your thumb. It should fracture the tessera cleanly.

Swimming pool table by Jon Suzuki, made with
cracked Spanish glazed ceramic tesserae,
by the direct method.

GLASS CUTTERS can be used with the thinner types of tesserae, such as Italian glass and ceramic, and the Asian porcelain. A small stick glass cutter costs less than 50¢ in most hardware stores. Hold the tessera between thumb and forefinger, or against a flat surface with your thumb. Run the small cutting wheel at one end of the cutter over the tessera where you plan to make the fracture. Pick up tessera and insert one edge of it into the small square groove below the cutting wheel of the cutter; the fracture line should be at a right angle to the wheel. With your other hand push down on the edge of the tessera away from the cutter; it should break evenly.

A word of caution when cutting stained glass; always wear leather gloves to prevent injury. A better method than the above for stained glass is with a mosaic cutter with adjustable blade, or of the *nail puller* or *wire cutter* type, where the cutting jaws meet.

BREAKING METHOD. It is almost impossible to determine the size and shape of pieces of tesserae when a breaking method is used; therefore it is not suitable for most projects. Tesserae can be placed between several sheets of newspaper, then broken with an ordinary hammer. They can also be broken by striking with a rubber-tipped hammer.

Cocktail table by Kenneth Weiss, made with thin cuts of Spanish glazed ceramic tesserae with hand-glazed ceramic tesserae for accents, by the direct method.

Cutting and shaping tesserae may seem difficult at first. But with a minimum of practice, the technique is quickly mastered. The possibilities for the creation of beautiful and interesting mosaics with various sizes and shapes of tesserae are then unlimited.

Backings, Edgings, and Hardware

When making a mosaic piece consideration must be given not only to the type of tesserae used, but also to the type of backing or frame, and edging. Tesserae can be adhered to many kinds of backing and types of edging; but the ones selected should help you fit the mosaic to its intended purpose.

To avoid errors which may be costly and bothersome, factors to predetermine include: The use and purpose of the mosaic, adaptability to weather if for outdoor use, resistance to heat or fire for certain uses, weight of materials used, smooth or rough surface or edges, and if a table, the placement of legs beneath the mosaic.

Whether you are making your own backing and edging, or purchasing at one of the larger mosaic stores a base with edging already attached, knowledge of backings and edgings, their suitability to your needs, and other factors, is important to know.

PLYWOOD BACKINGS are excellent for tesserae. Plywood is easy to work with, can be cut into any shape, and is relatively light in weight. It can be used for many purposes—table tops, counter surfaces, plaques, murals, trays, floors, and other. It permits the nailing or gluing on of edgings of various types. Legs can easily be mounted directly onto the plywood with flanges. It is easily mounted on walls and floors.

We recommend ¾″ five-ply exterior grade; it has the strength to give durability to your mosaic piece.

Plywood backings.

Before adhering tesserae to it, all plywood should be prepared with a brush coat of shellac on the front, back, and sides. The shellac, adequately applied, prevents moisture from seeping into the ply and warping it.

Regular finished lumber, such as pine or hardwoods, can also be used as backings.

Plywood backings are used in Projects 7, 8, 10, and 12.

Wrought-iron table frame
with backing.

Metal planter base.

MASONITE BACKINGS can be used for small mosaic pieces in much the same way that plywood is used, but it is not strong enough for larger pieces. It is usually ¼″ to ½″ thick, is porous, and has one smooth surface and one rough surface. It should be waterproofed on both sides with shellac. Tesserae should be applied to the smooth side, for the rough surface is very porous.

Masonite is not very satisfactory for mounting legs or edgings, for screw threads do not hold well in this fibrous material. It is strong enough in 12″ or 16″ squares for stacking tables and the like, but should be used only when frames are already provided, and the masonite can be secured in place by gluing down to the base with adhesive. Most of the foot square wrought-iron stacking table frames have an angle around the top frame into which the masonite can be fitted, and secured with mosaic adhesive or clips.

Bases or edgings prepared for masonite should be of wrought iron or metal, with the angle deep enough to hold the masonite thickness plus the tesserae. If a wooden edging is desired, have it made up like a picture frame so that the masonite backing can be fitted in and glued.

OLD FURNITURE BACKINGS. All kinds of old furniture—tables, counters, chests, etc.—can be used as a base for tesserae. These surfaces should be cleaned thoroughly. Remove all grease and wax with detergent, lighter fluid, alcohol, or turpentine. Remove loose paint with a plane or sandpaper. When the surface is clean, apply a thin brush coat of shellac.

ENAMEL SURFACES, when used as backings, should be clean of all foreign matter, especially grease. Few glues or adhesives adhere to non-porous surfaces; Italian mosaic adhesive is probably the most suitable.

 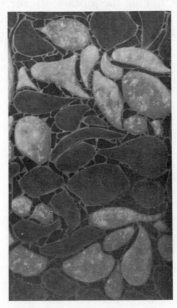

Outdoor vase (left) by Jack Kidder and James Dorris, made on a pottery backing with Italian glass tesserae, by the direct method. Cocktail table top or wall piece (right) by Alice Olson, made with hand-glazed enamel pieces on a copper backing, by the direct method.

PLASTIC BACKINGS are smooth and oily and need treating before adhesive is applied. Thoroughly clean surface, then rough up considerably with coarse sandpaper, before applying Italian mosaic adhesive.

LEATHER SURFACES should be removed from an old article you plan to use and a new backing substituted. If this is not practical, clean the leather surface thoroughly, give it a brush coat of shellac, and use Italian mosaic adhesive.

POTTERY, PLATES, AND PANS FOR BACKINGS. Beautiful and useful mosaic pieces can be made using old pottery, lamps, plates, pans, and other household wares. For example, the common pie pan or beer tray can be used as a backing for a mosaic tray, trivet, or plaque. The gauge of the tin or steel in the backing should be fairly thick or strong and not bend out of shape easily. But even if it is thin, the tesserae, when glued into place and cemented, will give it rigidity. If you are making a plaque, hangers can be purchased at a hardware store, and attached before making the mosaic. All foreign matter should be cleaned off the surface, then proceed as in Project 4, if you are working with a metal backing.

Wall hanging (left) by Jack Kidder and James Dorris, made on a gilded wooden backing, and plate or wall hanging (right) by Carmine D'Avino, made on a metal backing. Both are made with Italian glass tesserae, by the direct method.

MOSAIALIGHT SURFACES have been especially developed by its founders, Mosaic Crafts, and can be obtained with *Mosaialight* tesserae and special instructions. These backings are of plastic and permit light to shine through the backing and tesserae.

FINISHING BACKINGS. If the underside of the backing has become stained in making the mosaic, it should be cleaned off, then given either a coat of shellac or an appropriate stain. This will help preserve the wood, and prevent warping and moisture seepage into the mosaic.

WOOD EDGINGS, such as birch, walnut, oak, mahogany, and others, can be attached to plywood or other wood backings. They can be glued and clamped, or glued and nailed to cover the edge of the backing. Use a white casein glue, such as Elmer's or Rivit. If nailing, thin 17- to 20-gauge brads about 1″ long should be used, then the holes filled with plastic wood to match the color of the edging. Plastic wood comes in natural, oak, light and dark mahogany, and walnut.

The corners can be butted—one piece running across the end grain of the other, or mitered—as in picture frames—so no end grain shows. Mitering is not advisable in woods less than ¼″ thick.

Edgings should be mounted to the plywood or other wood with a rim above the surface deep enough to permit the tesserae top to come even with the top of the rim when they are mounted. Allow 3/16″ to 7/32″ for Italian or ceramic tesserae, and ¼″ for Byzantine.

Lumber yards will cut edgings. For Italian and Byzantine tesserae, ask for 1″ full by ¼″ or ⅛″, jointed one face (machine planed).

TESSERAE EDGINGS. A mosaic edge is easy to apply to a table, counter, or shelf, and it is usually less expensive than the conventional wood, brass, or wrought-iron edging. On a table or counter a tesserae edging can be blended with the top surface colors to give a pleasing overall effect. It is naturally not as strong as a wood or metal edging, but it will take average use. If an edging tessera becomes broken, with adhesive and a bit of recementing, it can be replaced.

If plywood is the surface material to be edged with tesserae, it is quite easy; the Italian and ceramic tesserae measure ¾″ square and fit perfectly over the edge of ¾″ plywood. Follow instructions given in Project 3.

Tesserae edgings can be laid to the edge of a wood table or counter surface, let dry and then cemented carefully. Place masking tape around the bottom edge before cementing, so the cement will not flow off.

METAL EDGINGS. Plywood is good backing when metal edges are used. Metal edgings may be wrought iron, aluminum or brass.

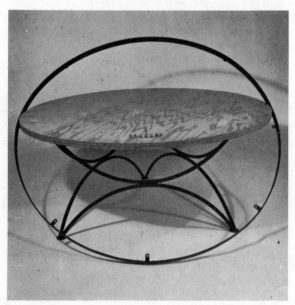

Wrought-iron table frame and edging, with
plywood backing.

Wrought-iron frames can be made inexpensively. Strip wrought-iron edging should be 1/16″ to ⅛″ thick and 1″ or more wide. Have metal tits brazed or welded to the bottom edge of the strip, then holes drilled through the tits for ¾″ screws. There should be enough tits to securely hold the plywood backing. Angle wrought iron should be 1/16″ to ⅛″ thick and 1″ wide, with 1″ or less under angle. Holes should be drilled through the under angle for ¾″ screws, for attaching the plywood backing. Wrought iron should be lacquered with a heavy coat (of the color you desire) to prevent iron rust.

Strip wrought iron or other metal edgings can be used by drilling holes along the sides and attaching the edging with flat-head screws to the plywood edge. The metal edging should be drilled so the screw tops and edging make an even surface. The disadvantage of this method is that the screw heads will show, and detract from the beauty of the mosaic piece.

Brass edging can be attached to any outgoing free form (a table with rounded outgoing or convex curves, and no sharp corners). Brass which is fairly thin, 1/16″ to 1/25″ thick, is more workable with the "pressure fit" technique; however, heavier grades can be used. The method of pressure fitting is fully described in Project 8.

HARDWARE: LEGS AND HANGERS. Deciding upon the type of hanger or leg to be used, if any, when planning your mosaic project will make it an integrated piece, and prevent later problems.

Depending upon the weight, wall murals and plaques can be hung with appropriate picture hooks or with ¾″ screws and strong picture wire.

The type of leg used and its placement under a table top should match and complement the overall design of the table. If the table has a metal or wood edging, the legs should match it. To achieve an overall effect of lightness and "floating," use a delicately shaped or tapered leg, and place well under the table at a slight angle, as in Project 8. If, for example, the table is a rectangle with heavy brass edging and you want it to have a heavy solid appearance, use a square solid brass leg.

Many mosaic and other stores have a large selection of legs in a variety of woods—walnut, birch, mahogany, oak, maple, ebony, fruitwood, and even exotic type woods—and shapes. Different tapers can be bought ready-made, or can be made with a wood turner. Legs can be finished to match the coloring of the table edging. A natural finish is satisfying and easy to keep; simply apply several coats of oil, such as tung oil or linseed oil, let dry, sand carefully, and repeat. Finish with a coat of clear furniture wax.

Combination legs of wood with brass ferrules can be used advantageously with either wood or brass table edges.

All sizes and shapes of brass, steel, copper, and aluminum legs can be obtained at mosaic supply outlets and many other stores. They are constructed in the same way as wooden legs, and can be attached to table tops by the use of flanges.

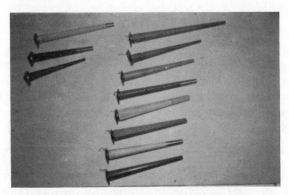

Series of wooden legs for table bases.

Flanges to attach to the table bottom come "straight" and "slanted." A single set of legs can be used either way, depending upon the flanges. Most wooden legs come with a machine bolt screwed into the top to help secure them in the flanges. Flanges are screwed to the table bottom with ¾" No. 7 or No. 8 round head steel screws. Various overall effects can be obtained, depending upon the type of flange and its placement. For example, slant flanges with legs placed well in from the table edge will give the table a "floating" effect.

CHAPTER 4

Adhesives

A number of adhesives, glues, cements, plasters, and concretes are advertised as "all purpose," but relatively few are suitable for mosaic work. While many of them will seemingly hold the tesserae to the backings, they weaken with time or under certain conditions, such as moisture, weather, cold, heat, and type of use the mosaic is put to. Specific adhesives are needed for tesserae with porous surfaces, and others for those with nonporous surfaces.

ADHESIVES FOR IMPERVIOUS, NONPOROUS TESSERAE. A rubber base type of adhesive, *Special Glass Adhesive,* is best for the impervious types of tesserae, such as Italian, Byzantine, or stained glass. This kind of adhesive dries rather slowly, and remains rubbery with age, rather than becoming hard. Hardness and dryness in adhesives indicate that adherence has been lost on impervious surfaces.

As discussed in the chapter on backings, those with porous surfaces should be shellacked, so they will not soak up the adhesive. It is also important that the backing surface be free of grease, water, or other foreign matter; tesserae should be wiped clean before placing in the adhesive.

Several of the larger mosaic retail and supply companies make up their own adhesives for impervious, nonporous surfaces. These usually sell for about 80¢ for two-ounce tubes, and $1.49 for five-ounce tubes. Two ounces of adhesive usually covers about 2½ to 3 square feet of surface. It is easy to use from the tube; simply squeeze a small ribbon of the adhesive over a small area, then place the tesserae; repeat the process until the entire surface is covered. Since the adhesive dries slowly, the tesserae can be pushed around and adjusted until properly placed. Edgings should always be covered with masking tape before putting down adhesive, for it is strong, and difficult to remove when it has dried. This technique of applying the tesserae to a base is called the direct method of application, and is discussed in a later chapter. It is also used in Projects 1, 3, 4, 5, 6, 7, 9, 11, and 12.

If you are dissatisfied with certain areas of your mosaic after laying the tesserae, and the adhesive has begun to dry, pour a solvent between the tesserae, and pry up with a small screw driver. Then reapply adhesive to the area and lay other pieces.

Impervious glass adhesive can be removed from the hands, frames, etc., with a common lighter fluid, nail polish remover, or carbon tetrachloride. Use carefully on the skin. If using carbon tetrachloride, have the room well ventilated and avoid breathing its fumes. These removers or solvents can be obtained at local drug stores and mosaic outlets.

The same type of adhesive is used when following the indirect or reverse method of application. When this technique is employed, since the adhesive dries more slowly than the cement, a strong bond is affected between the base, the cement, and the tesserae. This is important, for cements shrink slightly in drying and, alone, will not hold well to the backing. The indirect method is discussed later; it is also used in Projects 2, 8, and 10.

Large chemical companies, such as the Minnesota Mining and Manufacturing Co., usually manufacture adhesives for adherence of glass to glass or other nonporous surfaces, which may be obtained from their local distributors or mosaic outlets.

ADHESIVES FOR POROUS TESSERAE. While not as strong as the adhesives made for nonporous surfaces, *Ceramic Adhesives* made for porous materials are adequate for ceramic or clay-backed tesserae. They are spread evenly over a surface with a spreader or putty knife, then the tesserae placed into the wet adhesive. These adhesives are not transparent, so are not suitable when a design has been traced on the backing.

Ceramic adhesives are differently compounded and work on a different principle from that of the nonporous glass adhesives, which retain their adherent qualities without becoming hard. Ceramic adhesives are of a heavier, thicker consistency than the glass adhesives, dry in about 30 minutes, and become very hard when dry. A portion of it soaks into both the porous tesserae and the porous base, forming a hard, cement-like bond between the base and tesserae. This bond is adequate only when the two surfaces to be adhered are both porous.

The glass adhesive for impervious, nonporous surfaces is also good for the porous-backed tesserae. More adhesive should be used, for some will soak into the pores of the tesserae, weakening the bond if not adequately applied. For almost all mosaic projects the impervious, nonporous adhesive is more dependable and permanent. It compares favorably in cost to the porous adhesives; a five-ounce tube of the glass adhesive covers about the same area as a quart can of the porous type.

Ceramic adhesives cost about $2 a quart can, and can be bought at local tile contractors, hardware and mosaic stores. Among the satisfactory adhesives are Sure-Bond and Miracle Ceramic Cement. Solvents for these are usually listed on the product, but lighter fluid, gasoline, kerosene, or mineral spirits can be used, with care, as solvents or thinners.

WATER SOLUBLE ADHESIVES such as Rivet, Elmer's, etc., are inexpensive, and can be used where water or moisture is not a factor. These, however, should never be used if the rubber-base impervious, non-porous glass adhesives are available.

Mosaialight ADHESIVE is a special product developed for use with clear plastic backings and Italian glass tesserae. This process makes a lovely room divider or wall mural which permits light to shine through.

CHAPTER 5

Cements and Dyes

The term *cement* has been used consistently to refer to all materials—plaster, concrete, or grout—used to fill the areas between tesserae, or as a filler beneath the tesserae. Any number of materials may be used for these purposes: wall plaster, wall grout, bathroom grout, and other packaged mixes found in local hardware stores. Some of these may work adequately under average conditions; however, you may be taking a risk. A cement should be chosen to fit the purpose, use, and effect desired in your mosaic piece.

In selecting the cement to use consider the following:

Is the area large enough to warrant the use of less expensive cements?

Is the strength and hardness of the cement important to the mosaic?

Are weather conditions a factor?

What cement surface texture is desired—smooth, or a coarse or sandy pattern?

Do you plan to color the cement with a dye; is the color to be mixed evenly throughout?

Do you plan to use special cementing effects in the mosaic?

Mosaicists, probably since the beginning of their art, have experimented and worked to perfect a superior cement mixture which will hold the tesserae, resist weather and water, take dyes, have strength and smoothness. In earlier days when tables and murals were made by placing tesserae into heavy wet cement slabs, the cement mixture was vital; this method is still prevalent in Europe and in some areas of the United States. Even today, many mosaic artists and manufacturers guard the secrets of their cement contents, and continue experimenting to find a better cement. However, the search for a more perfect cement is less important with the American do-it-yourself methods of first gluing down the tesserae with adhesives, and using the cement as a filler.

MOSAIC GLASS CEMENT. The best mosaic cement for furniture and other household mosaic pieces is a special ready-mixed preparation carried by the larger mosaic stores. Manufactured for mosaic use, it does not contain sand or lime, is very dense, does not shrink, and is fine, smooth, and extremely hard when it dries. It can be dyed to strong colors without weakening its consistency. It comes already mixed and should be kept in its container until ready to use. At that time, place the cement in a mixing bowl, add water, pouring it down the side of the bowl a little at a time. Mix with your hand or a spoon, in a circular motion, until it is the consistency of thick pancake batter. The mixture should be smooth and creamy, without any lumps. Remove any air bubbles from the mixture by tapping the bowl gently on the table or floor; the bubbles will rise to the surface and break. The cement is then ready to use.

This special mosaic cement has been recommended in all the projects. It is sold by the pound, usually at about 80¢, but metal containers of 25 or 50 pounds can be bought for less. A pound covers approximately 1 to 2 square feet, depending on the closeness of the tesserae and the space to be filled in with the cement.

In addition to its obvious and usual uses as a filler between or an evener beneath tesserae, mosaic cement can be used to create other interesting and artistic mosaics.

A random mosaic table top can be made using the indirect method of application. Make a frame edging and clamp down securely to a flat surface. Spread a thin layer of axle grease on the flat surface inside the frame, and arrange tesserae face down. They may be placed as far apart as you wish them. For example, there can be small configurations of tesserae in the center only, with the remainder of the top cement. The table top may be given a marbleized effect by pouring colored dye mixtures in ribbons over the wet poured cement, then gently mixing the ribbons of dye into the cement with the forefinger. Colored sand placed on the flat surface before the cement is poured will give it a rough texture. Fine sand or marble dust mixed into the cement (1 part foreign matter to 2 parts mosaic cement) will give a rough texture. After arranging the tesserae on the flat surface, pour the cement over the back of the tesserae and smooth it out evenly within the frame. Apply adhesive to the backing, and place onto the wet cement within the frame. When the cement has dried, and the adhesive is holding the base to the dried cement and edging, turn the table top over. Pour water over the top, use a detergent if necessary, and scrub with copper scouring pads to remove the axel grease. When clean, wipe off with a sponge and water.

Another interesting technique uses cement to advantage, especially in wall murals where a bas-relief or dimensional effect is desired. Draw design onto a prepared base, then glue down tesserae. Into the large areas without tesserae pour mixed cement. Sprinkle dye pigment onto the wet cement and mix it in with your forefinger. Sand, colored glass, or other materials may also be added to the wet cement areas. To make the bas-relief, let cement partially dry, then add more cement to areas that are to be heightened.

PORTLAND CEMENT does not have the smoothness and nonshrinking qualities of special mosaic cements; neither does it take dyes as well. But for large projects where overall cost is a prime consideration, it is sometimes used. Mix in a proportion of 1 part cement to 3 parts fine grain sand for a mosaic grout. A finer mixture can be obtained by using marble dust as an aggregate in place of the sand.

This cement shrinks a little. When used as a grout between impervious tesserae, the drying and shrinking do not require special precautions. However, if it is used as a heavy bed, or as a complete mosaic slab several inches thick, then it must be strengthened and allowed to dry slowly. While the cement is wet, lay burlap or fine mesh chicken wire into it for reinforcement. To "cure" the cement and prevent shrinking or cracking, the slab should be covered with wettened newspapers or layers of burlap, and kept liberally dampened for several days.

CERAMIC GROUTS are manufactured for use on walls in tile bathrooms, kitchens, and hallways. Its composition is generally 80 to 90 per cent white Portland cement, with the balance lime or plaster of Paris; however, the Portland cement content of some prepared grouts runs as low as 50 to 60 per cent. It is usually obtainable in 25-pound bags.

Ceramic grouts may shrink slightly, but not as much as the straight Portland cement mixtures. They are easy to mix and use, but are not as hard as the glass mosaic or Portland cement mixtures when dry. They are softer, chalky, and can be chipped out from between the tesserae. These grouts do not take dye as readily as mosaic glass cement, or the Portland mixture.

MAGNESITE CEMENT is used by some mosaic specialists. It is composed of exychloride of magnesius. Lighter in weight than the Portland and special mosaic glass cements, it is not as water resistant. It is not ready mixed, but instructions can be obtained from the maker, Westvaco Mineral Products Division, New York City.

DYES of any type of finely ground mineral pigment can be used with mosaic cement. One to two full teaspoons of pigment per pound of cement gives a good intensity of color; a greater amount may weaken the cement. The dye color, when the cement has dried, will be 3 to 4 shades lighter than the dye mixture, so mix the dye to a darker shade than desired.

To mix the dye, measure pigment and place in a water glass. Add cold water and stir vigorously with a spoon until the dye is thoroughly mixed in. A wetting agent added to the dye mixture will help the dye to mix evenly throughout the cement, but it is not necessary. A wetting agent is a chemical which separates solids evenly in a fluid solution; it can be obtained at hardware and chemist stores.

When the dye is mixed into the water thoroughly, pour the solution down the side of the bowl of cement slowly and a little at a time. With a spoon or your hand, stir the dye into the cement until it is spread evenly throughout.

Mineral pigment dyes can be bought at mosaic stores, and cost from 15¢ to $1 per teaspoon, depending upon the color.

Dyes were used in Projects 8 and 10.

Steps in mixing dye and adding to cement: (top left) measuring dye, (top right) adding water, (center left) stirring to mix thoroughly, (center right) adding dye solution to dry cement, (bottom left) stirring to spread dye throughout, and (bottom right) adding water to cement.

FINISHING MATERIALS. After the mosaic is completed, the cement between the tesserae should be made water- and stainproof. Apply a coat of silicone polish over the mosaic surface. This can be obtained from mosaic suppliers; it costs less than $2 a pint.

PREPARATION OF TESSERAE BEFORE CEMENTING. The impervious, non-porous tesserae do not absorb water, and therefore require no special preparation before cementing. The cement, however, should be mixed to the consistency of heavy pancake batter, and then applied.

Porous tesserae should be soaked after they are placed in the adhesive, and before the cement is applied. Pour water over the table top and let stand 30 minutes. Tilt table to pour off any excess water, then apply cement. It should be mixed to the consistency of a light pancake batter. Place damp newsprint or cloths over the surface to prevent quick drying, which might powder and crack the cement. Since porous tesserae require so much watering, the base onto which they are glued should have a thorough waterproof coating of shellac or val-oil before the adhesive is applied.

CHAPTER 6

Direct and Indirect Methods of Application

Tesserae can be applied to backings or bases directly, piece by piece, then wet cement filled in the spaces in between; or they can be temporarily adhered to a sheet of kraft paper, then placed all at one time into the wet cement; this is the indirect method.

The direct method is probably simpler and easier for beginners. It has some disadvantages. If evenness of surface is important, tesserae will have to be chosen of uniform thickness. However, a slightly uneven surface reflects light beautifully. The gemlike qualities of Italian or Byzantine tesserae can create a texturally interesting, if uneven, surface. The unevenness will be so slight it will not affect even a table top.

DIRECT METHOD OF APPLICATION. Most tesserae come glued face down to foot-square sheets of paper. Soak the sheets in warm water for a few minutes; detergent may be added if you desire. Peel the pieces from the paper and dry them in a towel.

Prepare the backing or base for the mosaic piece. Cover all wood, brass or wrought-iron rims with masking tape to protect them from the adhesive and cement. Then plug all spaces where cement might run out with plastic wood or masking tape. Clean the surface, and if it is of wood, masonite or other porous substance, apply a brush coat of shellac. When the shellac is dry, draw the design directly onto the surface.

If the design calls for cut and shaped tesserae, some can be done before starting to lay the adhesive, or the design may be such that you will have to cut as you fill in the pieces.

The next step is adhering the tesserae. Squeeze a small amount of mosaic adhesive, from the 2-ounce or 5-ounce tubes, over as much area as you can cover with tesserae in twenty minutes. Place the tesserae, beveled side down, directly into the adhesive. Generally, if the design is a sunburst, start on the outside edges of the mosaic; if there are specific design areas, lay these before filling in the background. Continue squeezing adhesive over a small area, then laying the tesserae, until all the tesserae are in place. If you want to change the pieces in some places, pour a small amount of lighter fluid between the tesserae and with a small screw driver or similar tool pry up the ones you want to change. Rework by regluing.

If any of the adhesive gets onto your hands you can remove it with lighter fluid, acetone or benzine.

Let the adhesive dry at least 48 hours, or until the tesserae are firmly embedded and immovable. It will then be ready for cement; follow in-

72

structions given in the section on cement, or in Projects 1, 3, 4, 5, 6, 7, 9, 11, and 12, all of which were made by the direct method of application.

INDIRECT METHOD OF APPLICATION. In the indirect method, the tesserae are first mounted, face down, onto a sheet of kraft paper, and placed on the backing *after* the cement.

Soak the sheets of tesserae as in the direct method, remove them from the paper, and dry. Prepare the backing or base as given in the direct method.

Place a sheet of kraft paper onto the surface you are covering, trace an outline around the edge, then cut out around it. Sketch your design onto the paper, remembering that it will be in reverse, for the pieces are placed on it face down.

Using Duco or some other household-type cement, preferably water soluble, fill in the tesserae face down onto the paper, following your design.

Apply mosaic adhesive to the entire surface of the backing. Let it stand 4 to 7 minutes, until it becomes tacky. Mix the cement as instructed earlier. Pour the cement onto the surface and spread lightly with your hand, being careful to keep your hand from touching the adhesive.

Lift the paper holding the tesserae and place on top of the cement. You may need help with this. Or you can place a piece of cardboard on top of the tesserae, turn over so the paper side is up, then center the cardboard over the surface but not on the base itself. Slide out the cardboard, letting the tesserae fit into the cement inside the rim or edging.

Push the sheet around until it, and the tesserae, fit exactly into the frame. Press down into the cement and smooth the paper until it is level. Run a rolling pin vigorously over the paper, oozing out over the rim any excess cement. This will help push the Duco cement out between the tesserae and facilitate the peeling of the paper from them.

Wet the top of the paper with a sponge or damp cloth. Peel off the paper in strips. If it sticks to the tesserae and does not come off easily, redampen.

Run a rolling pin over the top of the tesserae to level them. If any pieces seem out of place, pull out and put back in a better position. When the pieces are in place as you want them, and the top is as smooth as possible, wipe it off with a damp cloth.

When the cement is partially dry, remove any bits of paper or dried Duco cement from between the tesserae with a toothpick. Fill in any holes made by the toothpick with cement. Let the top dry 12 to 20 hours.

Pour water over the top surface, scrub with copper scouring pads until clean, then dry it. Apply a coat of silicone polish and rub to give a finished look to the cement between the tesserae.

This indirect method of application is used in Projects 2, 8, and 10, and was explained fully in each of them.

CHAPTER 7

How to Design a Mosaic

Some may wish to create a mosaic piece using ideas of their own. Or a simplified version of a favorite painting, art object, travel poster or the like may be a source of inspiration for a design. There is no limit to the subject matter that can be put into mosaics.

For instance, one craftsman recently made a lovely wall mural depicting an Arabian riding a prancing horse; it was taken from a perfume advertisement. Another made a mosaic showing a cobblestone street in southern Italy. Interesting mosaics can be copied from postage stamp scenes, Indian designs, flowers, religious motifs, coat-of-arms, school subjects; anything that appeals to you.

It is important to remember that mosaic work has the inherent quality of stone. Its greatest beauty is in that quality. It is a medium in itself, and one should not try to "imitate" painting or any other medium. But its use is not limited by theme or subject matter; it can be equally interpretative in both "classic" and modern. Any theme you personally enjoy can be used for a mosaic pattern. An intricate theme of a painting, for example, can be simplified in your mosaic. Its character will be changed some when executed in tesserae, but the tone and feeling will be retained. It will be a distinctive mosaic, and your own, not just a copy of the model you used.

In selecting a design, think also in terms of the article you wish to make, and its size. It is advisable to make up the base or backing for your mosaic piece, or buy one of the many standard size bases already made up at a mosaic store, before purchasing tesserae, adhesive, cement, etc. After tracing or transferring your design onto the backing, you can more accurately determine the proper amount of materials.

Design drawn directly onto backing.

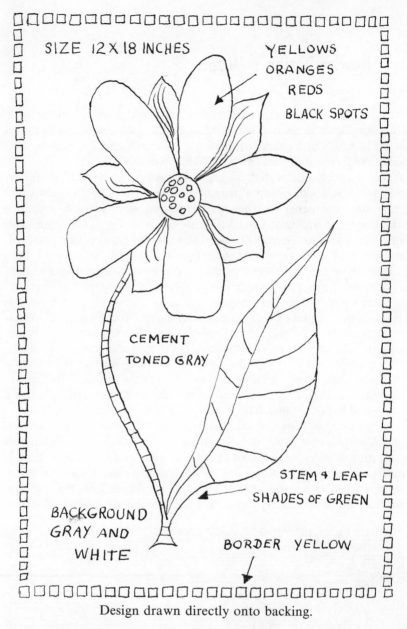

SIZE 12 X 18 INCHES

YELLOWS
ORANGES
REDS
BLACK SPOTS

CEMENT
TONED GRAY

STEM & LEAF
SHADES OF GREEN

BACKGROUND
GRAY AND
WHITE

BORDER YELLOW

Design drawn directly onto backing.

Prepare the base as discussed in the section on *Adhesives:* if it is porous, apply a brush coat of shellac to waterproof it; if it has an edging, cover this with protective masking tape.

There are several methods for transferring a design to a base.

DIRECT TRANSFER. You can pencil sketch or copy the design directly onto the base, or, if the design you are copying is the same size you desire your mosaic piece, use carbon paper and trace it. If it has to be enlarged for your piece, and you have difficulty with free-hand sketching, rule off a sheet of kraft paper the size of your base into equal spaces of ½″ to 1″ square. Enlarging your design proportionately, place outline dots or short lines in the squares. Roughly sketch in the design, using the dots or short lines to guide you. You can then transfer this design to the base by using carbon paper.

End table design incorporating personal initials, by Hans Scharff, made with Italian glass tesserae by the indirect method.

INDIRECT TRANSFER. If your mosaic piece is being made by the indirect method of application, as explained in a later section, then the design should be outlined on kraft paper *in reverse*. It will then be as you want it when the tesserae, which have been adhered to the kraft paper top side down, have been placed into the wet cement and the paper removed from the top side.

The materials used in turning a design into a mosaic will greatly determine its appearance when completed. In styling it, carefully consider the choice of colors, size and kind of tesserae, techniques in laying the tesserae, and the finishing of the mosaic.

COLOR SELECTION. Regardless of the kind of tesserae used, the range of color can be almost as extensive as from the palette of an artist. There is less frustration in making a mosaic because the colors can be seen immediately; you do not have to mix them. But if the mosaic is to be aesthetically appealing, you will have to give the same consideration to color that an artist does when working with his oil paints.

A practical approach is to secure color charts of the various tesserae. Tesserae colors vary in intensity with manufacturers, so look at all of them; you will have a greater color selection that way. For instance, the Pelv Italian glass tesserae come in 60 to 80 colors, and the Continental Italian glass tesserae totals between 48 and 60 colors. Combined, you have over 120 colors to choose from, with many shadings of a single color.

Byzantine tesserae are made in over 7,000 colors. About 120 to 140 are available in the larger mosaic stores; however, additional colors can be ordered. Marble tesserae are limited by nature to 8 to 10 shadings. Ceramic tesserae come in 20 to 60 colors, but their range within a color is limited.

Portion of pattern tracing, showing size and shape
of cuts of tesserae.

SIZE AND KIND OF TESSERAE. Very effective combinations of tesserae, such as Italian and Byzantine, together with marble—and their inherently different surface textures—can enhance the design of some mosaics. The larger porcelain tesserae can be effective when a certain boldness of design is wanted.

Tesserae are marketed in only a few standard sizes, but they can be cut and shaped. Very small cuts of tesserae give a mosaic a degree of "realism"; large bold cuts give it an "impressionistic" feel. This is exactly like the painter who uses small delicately blended brush strokes to achieve a realistic portrait, and the bold strong strokes of a brush as found in a Van Gogh.

TECHNIQUES. In some designs of linear concept the emphasis is on outline, although color values cannot be ignored. To illustrate: A simple outline of a fish might be set in with black stones to give it emphasis, with any pleasing color used for the body. To keep the strong linear outline, fill in the background with a color very low in key, such as white or light gray, so the fish will stand out. A *few* pieces of slightly deeper gray and red can be added to the background to break the monotony—the dash of salt needed to give it life. If the background tesserae are elongated and narrow, they can also give a sense of movement within themselves. The geometric quality of a rhythmic pattern adds its own quality of beauty and strength.

Some mosaics can be made effective by a symbolization of the shapes of tesserae. For example, a design of New York City's skyline with the East River in the foreground could use long thin chips for the water, squares for the embankment, rectangles for the buildings, and triangles for the sky. The shaping of the tesserae, along with the color shadings of the tesserae, is your "paint brush."

The surfaces of the various kinds of tesserae can also be used to advantage. The Italian tesserae has a smooth side, the face, but the pieces vary in thickness. If they are applied to the backing by the direct method, the top will not have the smooth appearance the indirect method will give. Byzantine does not have a smooth surface, and light will reflect from the individual pieces at many angles. The reflection will be slightly less if the indirect method is used.

This brief discussion of styling will stimulate ideas to experiment with in creating a mosaic of your own design. By combining materials, colors, sizes and shapes of tesserae chips, realistic, impressionistic, abstract, and nonobjective effects can be obtained. Creating your own mosaic can be aesthetically satisfying and also worth-while.

CHAPTER 8

Mosaic Walls and Panels

Magnificent murals can be added to any wall, or it can be covered with a plain or patterned mosaic. The tesserae can be applied to any part of any type of wall, indoors or outdoors.

The glass types of tesserae, and some types of ceramic and porcelain tesserae, are ideally suited for murals and plain walls. Since the surface of these tesserae is impervious or semi-impervious, dirt does not stick to it, it cannot fade, and it will not deteriorate like wallpaper and painted surfaces.

Abstract wall mural by Valerie Clairbout, made with marble tesserae on a painted background, by the direct method (not grouted).

The initial expense may be greater than for other wall coverings, but in the long run a mosaic wall surface is economical in upkeep and replacement, and much more beautiful than the ordinary wall.

In planning a wall mural or mosaic, refer to the preceding sections on

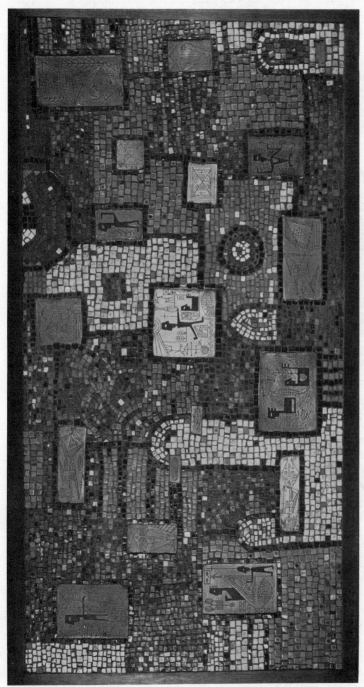

Wall mural by P. D. Halloman, made with hand-fired glazed ceramic tesserae and hand-etched and glazed tile insets, by the direct method.

the various materials for a greater discussion of kinds, quantities, and application. Below are several easy methods of surfacing walls.

DIRECT METHOD OF SURFACING WALLS. The Italian glass tesserae and the ceramic types of tesserae that usually come glued face down to thin paper in one-foot-square sheets are especially convenient for this method of application. The individual pieces are usually ¼″ thick and ¾″ square; 225 pieces, all of one color, come glued to each square-foot sheet. After the wall is prepared, the tesserae can be placed on it by sheet.

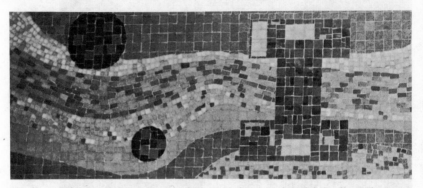

Wall panel of contour map and house plan made with Italian glass tesserae by the direct method. Panel pattern includes a house and a stream running beneath it, and trees and lawn.

To add color, geometrical designs, or patterns, pry up the tesserae from the sheets, where color is to be added. Reglue tesserae of other colors into these spots with Duco or a water soluble paste. Line up the sheets of tesserae on a flat surface in the position they will take on the wall.

If the pattern or design is intricate, trace or draw it onto kraft paper, then adhere the tesserae face down to the paper with Duco or a water soluble paste. To remove tesserae from original paper backing, soak in warm water for 15 minutes, peel pieces from the paper, and dry.

To prepare the wall, clean thoroughly, remove all loose matter with a wire brush, patch any holes with a wall plaster, then wipe down with a clean cloth. If it is oily, use a detergent or turpentine on it, then wipe. An exceedingly rough wall should be given an undercoat of strong plaster to smooth it off. If it is of a very porous material, coat with shellac, and let dry.

Starting at the bottom of the wall, smear a thick coat of mosaic adhesive over an area of about one and a half feet square. Let it dry for a few minutes until it becomes tacky, then place a foot square of tes-

Abstract wall mural by Valerie Clairbout, made with Italian glass tesserae by the direct method (not grouted). Small cuts, placed side edge up, give it the textural effect.

serae into the adhesive. Apply adhesive to the same size area immediately above, let it become tacky, then place another foot square of tesserae. The tesserae will have a tendency to slide down if you start at the top. Continue this process until the wall is covered. Let the adhesive and mosaic sheets dry 24 to 48 hours.

Soak the paper backings with a sponge or cloth full of water. After about five minutes of soaking, peel the paper from the tesserae.

If any of the adhesive has oozed up between or onto the tesserae, soften with lighter fluid or carbon tetrachloride (ventilate the room well if using the latter), and scrape off with a penknife or razor blade.

When the mosaic is clean mix the cement, with dye if desired, to a consistency of very heavy pancake batter. Take a handful of cement at a time and, beginning at the top of the wall, rub it over the tesserae, using the pressure of your hand to force the cement into all the spaces between the pieces.

When all the spaces are filled, wipe the excess cement from the surface, taking care not to wipe it out of the spaces between the tesserae. Do not try to clean the wall completely at this time. Let the cement dry several hours, then wipe with a slightly damp cloth until no excess cement remains on the surface of the tesserae. Let the wall dry 6 to 8 hours.

Wipe down the wall with water; scrub with copper scouring pads if necessary. When it is perfectly clean, let it dry for several hours. Apply a waterproofing silicone polish (to make the cement stainproof); when dry, polish with a dry cloth.

INDIRECT METHOD OF SURFACING WALLS. This method is particularly suitable to the porous types of tesserae, such as ceramic and semi-impervious porcelain. The sheets of tesserae are placed directly into the cement, rather than into an adhesive. The pores of the tesserae backs soak up a certain quantity of the cement and form a bond.

Rub down the wall with a wire brush or wash with muriatic acid to remove loose cement, dirt and foreign matter. If the wall surface is smooth and of a nonporous material, rough it up, so that the new coat of plaster or cement will adhere to the old surface.

A strong plaster mixture, ceramic wall tile grout, or a wall cement may be used. Most of these can be obtained from a hardware store or tile contractor. Make certain whichever you use will bind to the wall material, will not shrink appreciably, will give good adherence to the tesserae, and will not easily chip away from between the tesserae. Special mosaic cement may also be used.

Mix the wall cement as directed, and spread it over the wall surface. Smooth it with your hand or a flat board. Starting at the bottom, place the sheets of tesserae into the cement. Even them off, and smooth flat with your hand or a board. Let the cement dry 12 to 24 hours.

Soak the paper backing with water, then peel off the paper. Where regrouting is necessary, mix a new batch of cement, and push this between the tesserae with a board or other flat surface. Then finish the wall as outlined in the direct method of surfacing above.

Abstract mural (partial) by Larry Argiro, made with Italian glass tesserae, by the indirect method. Artist shown with tesserae partially glued to kraft paper.

DIRECT PLACEMENT METHOD. This method is very easy, but somewhat tiring, since you are working on a vertical surface. If you are making a design or pattern with the tesserae, draw or sketch in the outline on the wall. Follow complete procedure given for the direct method of surfacing, except that the tesserae are placed piece by piece, and according to your design, directly into the adhesive on the wall surface, instead of by sheets of 225 at a time. You will, of course, need to remove the tesserae from the paper backing, and dry them before applying to the wall, ridged side into the adhesive.

VENEER METHOD. You may use a plywood backing and edging, making your mosaic wall piece in the same way as a table top. When completed, mount it on the wall with cement nails or bolts.

The above methods may be used for any other vertical surfaces, such as doors and cabinet fronts. If the surface to be covered is outdoors, select adhesive, cement, and tesserae that will withstand the elements.

CHAPTER 9

Mosaic Floors and Walks

Mosaic floors and walks are easily made, and have lasting strength and beauty that few if any other materials can match. Methods are given in brief form here, but the general information and instructions given in the preceding sections, as to the use of materials and their qualities, should be followed carefully. If this is done, your floor or walk will turn out beautifully.

The chapter on tesserae describes the various kinds thoroughly. Since the clay-backed ceramic tesserae chip easily, they are not suitable for floors and walks. If you use the direct method of application and Italian glass tesserae, select individual pieces of uniform thickness, for the Italian glass varies slightly.

The chapter on cements gives information on kinds and uses. Mosaic cement is advisable if the floor area is small. However, if the area to be covered is large, and if you use the indirect method of application which requires a greater quantity of cement, it will be more economical to use ordinary floor or walk cement. In this case the cement mixture should be strong—1 part cement to 2 to 4 parts fine white sand or marble dust. Use a dye mixture, if any, sparingly. Keep the floor dampened with wet burlap, or wet newspapers, to prevent fast drying, and to prevent the cement from shrinking and cracking.

Old floors should be cleaned thoroughly of dirt, foreign matter, or grease, and smoothed with a plane or sander if they are uneven. If the indirect method of application of tesserae is used, plug any holes to prevent the cement or grout from flowing into them.

DIRECT METHOD. Shellac the floor thoroughly, let it dry, then draw your design directly onto it. Cover a small area with mosaic adhesive, and place tesserae directly into it, following your pattern. Continue working a small area at a time until all the tesserae are in place. Let the adhesive dry 24 to 48 hours. Mix the cement, with dye if desired, to a consistency of very heavy pancake batter. Pour this mixture over the floor, and rub it into the spaces between the tesserae. Wipe off the excess cement and let the mosaic dry 6 to 12 hours. Pour water on the floor and clean with copper scouring pads. Waterproof with silicone polish.

INDIRECT METHOD. This method gives a smoother floor surface, and the uneven types of tesserae can be used with little difficulty.

Draw your design to size on kraft paper, then cut into one-foot squares. Following this design, glue the tesserae face down to the paper with an "easy" type of adhesive, such as Duco or a water soluble paste.

Spread a thick layer of mosaic adhesive over the floor, using heavy cardboard or a piece of flat-edged wood. Let it dry 5 to 10 minutes.

Mix the cement, with dye if desired, to a consistency of heavy pancake batter. Pour it over the adhesive, and smooth. The cement layer should be at least as thick as the thickest tesserae you are using.

Lay the squares of tesserae, according to your design, into the wet cement, with the paper side up. Smooth each square as you lay it, by running your hand over the surface of the paper. Let the cement dry 12 to 24 hours, then pour water over the paper squares, let soak a while, then peel the paper from the tesserae. If the cement did not ooze up evenly to the tops of the tesserae, mix a small amount of cement, and rub it into the spaces. Let it dry.

Clean the mosaic floor with water and copper scouring pads, dry, then waterproof the cement with a coat of silicone marble polish applied to the floor surface. Polish with a dry cloth.

VENEER METHOD. This method obviates the necessity of repairing badly damaged or uneven floors. Mat paper or cardboard in the low spots so the veneer backings will not bend or rock appreciably when they are covered with tesserae and laid on the floor.

Cut thin sheets of plywood or masonite in large squares or rectangles to fit the floor. Apply the tesserae to the backing, as in making a mosaic table top. When completed, secure the veneer sections to the floor with adhesives or screws.

CASTING METHOD. This method can be used for either floors or walks, indoors or out. Make a regular cement frame or form, pour in the cement and, using the indirect method, lay sheets of tesserae. When the cement is dry, remove the paper and the forms.

Individual steps of a walk may be laid in individual forms. Place the tesserae face down onto a greased surface within the frame, then pour cement over the backs of the tesserae and level. Strengthen the cement block by adding small mesh chicken wire or burlap while the cement is still wet. When the cement block is dry, remove it from the wooden form, turn over, and remove the greased surface. The mosaic top will be smooth. A series of these makes an interesting walk.

PART 3: Patterns

Abstract Girl

By Carmine D'Avino for The
Mosaic Gallery.

A 3' x 1' *Mosaialight* wall
panel, illuminated by back
lighting. Made with Italian
glass tesserae, using the special *Mosaialight* backing and
the direct method of application. Figure and background
were done with ¼" cuts; border with full ¾" tesserae.
Some tesserae will have to be
cut and shaped to fit into the
design. Figure was done in
brilliant reds, oranges, yellows, and black; background
and border in light lavenders
and grays.

Pattern 1

Pattern 2

Star and Spiral Tray

By John Kidder and James Dorris for The Mosaic Gallery.

A 20″ diameter tray, made with Italian glass tesserae, using the direct method of application. Some tesserae will have to be cut and shaped to fit into the design. Can be constructed in any contrasting colors desired, using ¼″ cuts closely fitted together. It may also be used as a wall decoration, or an end table with solid brass tripod base.

Pomegranate Tree

By John Kidder and James Dorris.

A 5′ x 2′ *Mosaialight* wall panel, framed in 2″ square oiled walnut, illuminated by back lighting. Made with Italian glass tesserae, using the special *Mosaialight* backing and the direct method of application. Some tesserae will have to be cut and shaped to fit into the design. The pomegranates were done in brilliant reds and oranges; the leaves in green, bordered with black for accents; and the trunk in deep browns and beiges. The background was done in mixtures of off-white and grays.

Pattern 3

Pattern 4

Star and Sphinx Wall Hanging

Star and Sphinx Wall Hanging

By John Kidder and James Dorris.

A 54″ x 24″ rectangle with a natural finish oak edge. Made with ¼″ and ⅛″ cuts of Italian glass tesserae, using the direct method of application. Some tesserae will have to be cut and shaped to fit into the design. Any combination of colors may be used for this design.

Indian Design Coffee Table

By Jon Suzuki for Mosaic Crafts.

A 40″ diameter table bound in brushed brass. Made with Italian glass tesserae, using the indirect method of application. Any contrasting colors are suitable.

Pattern 5

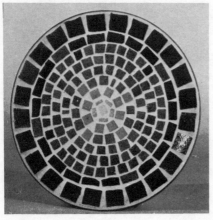

Pattern 6

Sunburst Tray

By Edwin A. Hendrickson for Mosaic by the Numbers, Inc.

An 8½″ diameter aluminum tray, made with Italian glass tesserae, using the direct method of application. Some tesserae will have to be cut and shaped to fit into the design. Any combination of colors may be used.

Tulip Tray

By Edwin A. Hendrickson for Mosaic by the Numbers, Inc.

An 8½″ diameter aluminum tray, made with Italian glass tesserae, using the direct method of application. Some tesserae will have to be cut and shaped to fit into the design. Any combination of colors may be used.

Pattern 7

The Man

By Carmine D'Avino for Batea Trading Co.

A 10″ diameter brass tray made with Italian glass tesserae, using the direct method of application. Some of the tesserae will have to be cut and shaped to fit into the design. The background was done in light shades of beige and pink; with contrasting colors for the figure.

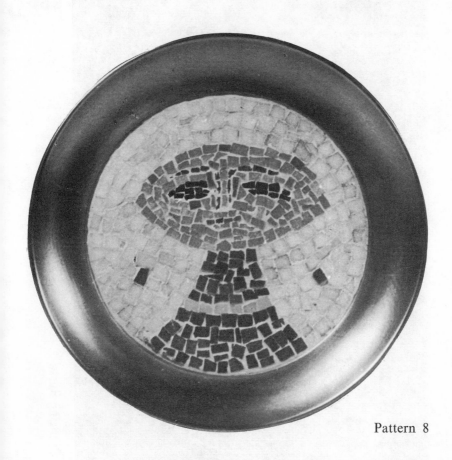

Pattern 8

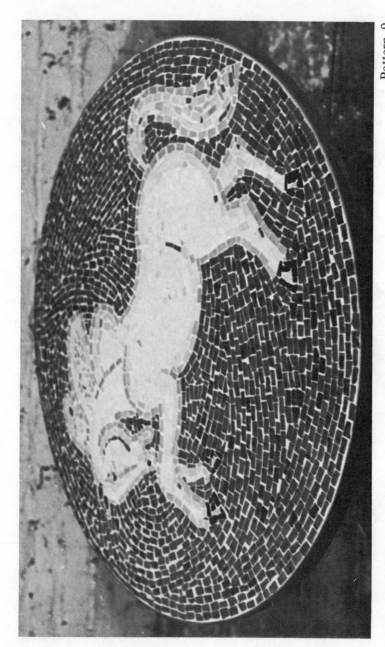

Prancing Horse

Prancing Horse

By Clements Gregory for The Mosaic Gallery.

A 32" diameter table top with oiled walnut edge. Made with Italian glass tesserae, using the indirect method of application. Some tesserae will have to be cut and shaped to fit into the design. The horse was done in pink wheat and shadings of off-white grays; and the background in ½" cuts of Venetian red.

Flying Bird Tray

By Clements Gregory for Batea Trading Co.

A tray, table top or wall hanging made with Italian glass tesserae, using the direct method of application. Some tesserae will have to be cut and shaped to fit into the design. Select a pale background with any combination of brilliant colors for the figure.

Pattern 10

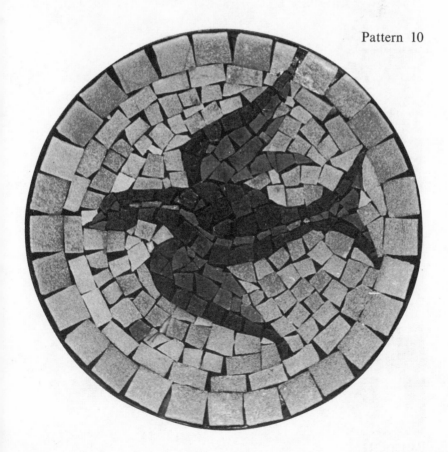

Mosaialight Abstract

By Samuel Kaner for The Mosaic Gallery.

A 5′ x 1′ *Mosaialight* panel illuminated by back lighting. Made with Italian glass tesserae, using the special *Mosaialight* backing and the direct method of application. Some tesserae will have to be cut and shaped to fit into the design. It was constructed in various brilliant shades.

Pattern 11

Pattern 12

Nude

By Edwin A. Hendrickson for Mosaic Crafts.

A 30″ x 30″ wall panel or table top with rubbed oak edging. Made with Italian glass tesserae, using the indirect method of application. Some tesserae will have to be cut and shaped to fit into the design. Subtle blending of colors and tiny cuts will give a rounded quality to the figure. The background is plain.

Pattern 13

Woman's Face

By Clements Gregory for Bon Bazar.

A 20″ diameter mosaic on masonite, no edging, for wall hanging. Made with Italian glass tesserae, using the direct method of application. Some tesserae will have to be cut and shaped to fit into the design. The face was done in beiges, off-white pinks, and wheat shades. Background was done in a mottled darker color.

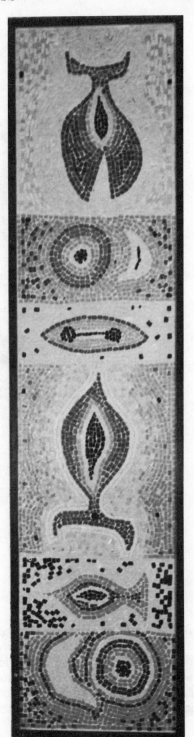

Fish Abstract

By Carmine D'Avino for Mosaic Crafts.

A 72″ x 20″ wall mural bound in 1″ wide oiled walnut. Made of brilliant Byzantine tesserae, using the indirect method of application. Some tesserae will have to be cut and shaped to fit into the design. Any combination of colors may be used for this mosaic.

Pattern 14

Pattern 15

Free Form Logo of a "Home Show"

By John Kidder and James Dorris for Mosaic Crafts.

A 48″ x 30″ walnut-edged free form. Made with Italian glass tesserae, using the direct method of application. Not cemented. Some tesserae will have to be cut and shaped to fit into the design. The background and center square were done in ½″ cuts of pink wheat; the center circle in ¼″ cuts of black; and the center design in ½″ and ¼″ cuts of red.

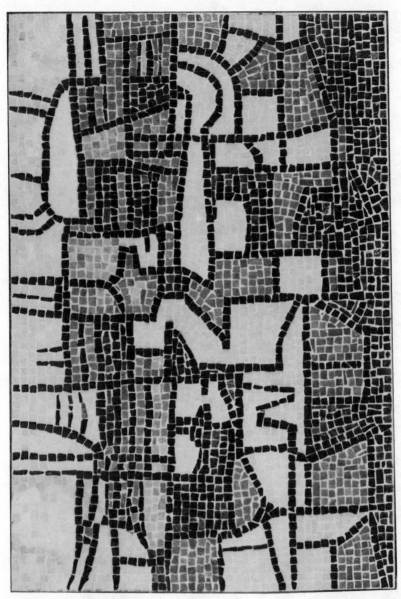

Pattern 16

Abstract

By George Morrison for The Mosaic Gallery.

A 48″ x 24″ wall hanging edged in limed oak. It was made with ¼″ cuts of Italian glass tesserae, using the direct method of application, in shades of black, gray and white.

The Birds

The Birds

By John Kidder and James Dorris for The Mosaic Gallery.

A 54″ x 24″ wall panel bound in polished brass. Made with Italian glass tesserae, by the indirect method of application. Some tesserae will have to be cut and shaped to fit into the design. May be made in any combination of colors.

Greek Key Coffee Table

By John Kidder and James Dorris for Mosaic Crafts.

A 42″ diameter table bound in satin brass. Made with Italian glass tesserae, using the indirect method of application. May be made in any color combination.

Pattern 18

Pattern 19

Fruit Bowl Abstract

By Carmine D'Avino for The Mosaic Gallery.

A 3' x 2' wall hanging edged in oiled mahogany, made with Byzantine tesserae, using the indirect method of application. Some tesserae will have to be cut and shaped to fit into the design. Done primarily with reds, oranges, and blacks for figure; and a pastel color for the background.

Pattern 20

Cat

By Hans Scharff.

A 40″ x 40″ wall hanging made with Italian glass tesserae, using the indirect method of application. Some tesserae will have to be cut and shaped to fit into the design. It may be made in dark shades of any color, with white for contrast; it may be edged in either wood or brass.

Sources of Supply

Tesserae and equipment can often be purchased in the Arts and Crafts departments or Hobby Shops of larger department stores. They usually stock the ordinary types of tesserae, such as Italian glass, Italian ceramic, and Asian porcelain. Their color selection may not be great.

Many art supply stores and crafts and hobby shops carry tesserae and equipment.

Several large mail order houses carry tesserae and equipment and list them in their catalogs. Other mail order houses specialize in arts and crafts; some of these advertise nationally. All will be pleased to furnish full price lists.

You may also locate sources of supply by consulting the classified telephone directory in your community. Look in the yellow pages under "Arts and Crafts" or, in larger cities, under "Mosaics." Local art schools may be able to furnish names of possible suppliers. Tile contractors may know where the ceramic tesserae can be purchased.

If you are not able to locate suppliers, the author will furnish lists; write to him in care of the publisher.